Shakespeare's Life and Times

Ray Mackay

Macmillan Publishers

First published 1992
Reprinted 1994

ISBN 962 03 0649 X

Published by
MACMILLAN PUBLISHERS LIMITED

Companies and representatives throughout the world

Printed in Hong Kong

ACKNOWLEDGEMENTS

The author and publisher would like to thank the following for permission to reproduce copyright material in the book:

Aquarius Picture Library; The British Film Institute; The Chung Ying Theatre Company; The Photomas Index; Ringo Chan; The Shakespeare Centre Library; The Tom Holte Theatre Photographic Collection; Virgin Films.

Original illustrations by K.Y. Chan

Every effort has been made to trace copyright, but in the event of any accidental infringement where it has proved untraceable, we shall be pleased to come to a suitable arrangement with the rightful owner.

For Jo

'Love goes toward love, as schoolboys from their books
But love from love, toward school with heavy looks'

Romeo and Juliet (Act II, Scene I)

and Rowan

'A horse! a horse! my kingdom for a horse'

Richard III (Act V, Scene IV)

CONTENTS

I
THE ELIZABETHAN AGE

'I can smile, and murder while I smile... And frame my face to all occasions'

Henry IV Part III (Act III, Sc II)

1. INTRODUCTION

William Shakespeare was born on April 23rd, 1564, and he died on April 23rd, 1616. He had written 38 plays in the space of 22 or 23 years, in addition to a large number of poems.

William Shakespeare

DID YOU KNOW?
Shakespeare died on his 52nd birthday.

The name Shakespeare originally meant a soldier – one who shakes a spear.

At that time, it was normal for a play to be performed only three or four times and very few plays were ever printed. Shakespeare had to write quickly and it is very probable that he wrote for money rather than for any idea about future fame and glory. But this only makes him more interesting.

In 1623 the first collection of his plays (containing only 36) was printed. His friends realized that he was a great writer but they could never have imagined that hundreds of years later people all over the world would know the name William Shakespeare.

In this book we shall explore how a simple man who never went to university became one of the greatest dramatists in the world. We shall look at the society he lived in, the things he wrote about, the life he led and the effect he had on the world of literature.

2. BACKGROUND

Shakespeare was born in the town of Stratford-upon-Avon. Look at the map below and follow the instructions to find out where Stratford-upon-Avon is. Mark it on your map.

INSTRUCTIONS:
1. *Follow the road out of London which takes you west and slightly north. You arrive at...where?*
2. *Take the road which goes north-west from there. Which city are you travelling towards?*
3. *Stop half-way. You are now in Stratford-upon-Avon.*

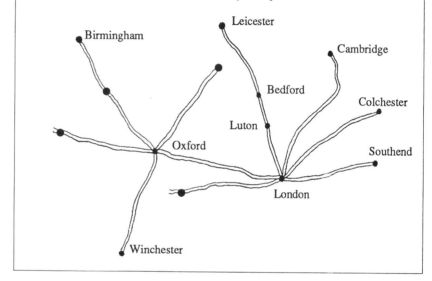

Shakespeare's father, John Shakespeare, moved to Stratford in about 1550. At that time, Stratford was a small town of about 2,000 people. It was important only because of its bridge across the river Avon. Try to imagine what it was like . . . the houses were made of wood and usually had thatched roofs – roofs made of straw. The main streets were full of trees and there were animals everywhere – cows, sheep, goats, pigs, horses, donkeys. The streets were very muddy when it rained and dusty when it was dry. There was always a lot of rubbish lying about. There were no street lights, of course, and the fastest means of communication was the horseman. Children went to school at seven in the morning and came back home at five in the afternoon, with two hours off for the midday meal. People didn't have clocks or watches. The town bell rang at six in the morning to wake people up and again at eight in the evening to tell them that they should be at home.

3

ACTIVITY:

Look at the drawing below. This is a typical street scene of the 16th century but there are five mistakes in the picture. Working in groups of 4/5, can you find the five mistakes?

TALKING POINT:

What are the differences between your school and the kind that Shakespeare might have gone to?

When he was about 15 he left school. We don't know what he did after that but it is important to remember that the idea of childhood was very different then: a 15 year-old boy was a man who had to work. The next thing we know for sure about William Shakespeare is that, on November 28th, 1582, he married Anne Hathaway, aged 26. Six months later a daughter, Susanna, was born.

John Shakespeare was a glove-maker and wool-dealer, which means that a lot of his time would have been spent looking at animals and their skins. It is very likely, therefore, that William Shakespeare spent his early life helping his father to kill and skin animals. We know that young William went to the free grammar school where he would have been taught Latin, which was the language of the Romans and, at that time, still the language of academics, the Church and the State. He probably didn't get to study many books in English because printing had only been available in England for just over a hundred years and his school would not have had a great deal of money to buy these new books. Schools then were very different from those of today. If a child misbehaved he or she was given the birch. On the following page you can see what a birch looked like – it was made of pieces of birch wood tied together. You can imagine what it felt like!!

A birch

A man called Henry Peacham wrote a very interesting description of some of his teachers:

'I know one who in winter would, on a cold morning, whip his boys for no other purpose than to get himself a heat. Another beat them for swearing, and all the while swore himself, with horrible oaths.'

ACTIVITY:
Read the following letter which a young girl has written to the problem page of a magazine.

TALKING POINT:
Shakespeare had to marry because Anne Hathaway was expecting a baby. In Elizabethan England, this situation was not unusual. What would happen today in your society if the same situation occurred? How would the young couple feel? How would their parents feel?

Dear Mary,

I'm writing to you because I don't know what else to do. I'm 17 years old and I've been going out with a boy for a year now. My parents like him very much but they don't want us to get engaged until I have finished school and gone to university. I take my final school exams next year. The problem is that I have discovered that I'm pregnant. I haven't told anyone, not even Dave, my boyfriend. I'm very frightened that if I tell my parents, the news will destroy them because I'm their only child and they really want me to go to university and get a degree. Please tell me what to do.

Yours sincerely,

Very Worried

IN GROUPS:
Try to suggest some of the things that this young girl should do. Make a list of the things she should do:
a) _____
b) _____ etc.

INDIVIDUALLY:
Now write a response to the girl. Begin: Dear Very Worried.

DISCUSSION:
What are the problems that occur in families when one of the parents has to leave home to work somewhere else? Does this happen in your society? What are the causes?

The next seven years are often called 'the lost years' because no one knows what Shakespeare did during this time. It is safe to assume that he read a lot and also that he saw some of the plays performed by the travelling groups of players who toured England. The next thing we know is that he was in London, possibly having followed a group of actors. We don't know exactly when he went to London but it must have been round 1589 because two years later he was writing great drama and that is something that is not learned in a moment. By that time he had three children and was 25 years of age. What could have made him suddenly give up his life in Stratford and move to London where he would be poor and in much greater danger from illness, disease and violent crime? No one knows. Perhaps it was a family quarrel; perhaps he felt that he had to go and seek his fortune; perhaps he realized that he was good with language and could earn money through writing plays; perhaps he met someone who suggested that he should go . . . We don't know but we are very glad that he did because London was going to turn him into one of the greatest dramatists in the world.

3. EXPLORERS AND PIRATES

ACTIVITY:
As you read the following passage, fill in each blank with one of the words from the list below.

developing	begun	were	came	sent
found	born	conquer	managed	buy	became
destroyed	sinking	open	was	discovered

DID YOU KNOW?
In 1494 Spain and Portugal made the Treaty of Tordesillas which divided the whole world outside Europe between them. In 1580, Philip II in Spain conquered Portugal and so, apart from Europe, the whole world belonged to Spain.

Queen Elizabeth I _____ to the throne in 1558, six years before Shakespeare was _____. She very quickly _____ popular with the people of England because it _____ obvious to everyone that, under her leadership, England was _____ into a strong nation, peaceful and wealthy at home, powerful overseas. Perhaps it was because of such peace in England that men like John Hawkins and Francis Drake became bored and went to sea on great journeys of adventure. At first, these journeys _____ attempts to _____ up trade routes to other markets so that England could _____ and sell goods, but soon they became much more violent as English ships began attacking, robbing and _____ other ships. The age of the pirates had _____. The greatest sea powers in Europe at that time were Spain and Portugal. Christopher Columbus, working for the King and Queen of Spain, had _____ America in 1492 and, since that time, the Spanish had become very rich due to the silver which they _____ in Mexico and Peru. The English sailors began attacking the Spanish treasure ships coming from the New World and this led England into a war with Spain. In 1588, the Spanish _____ an Armada of 130 ships to attack and _____ England. They failed and huge storms _____ many of their ships. Only 67 Spanish ships _____ to return safely.

This is the background against which the young dramatist William Shakespeare began his writing career and it is not surprising to discover that his early plays are concerned with violence and patriotism. No one is really sure exactly when, or in what order, Shakespeare wrote his plays, but his first play was probably *Titus Andronicus* (1589/90).

4. SHAKESPEARE'S FIRST PLAY

TALKING POINT:
Someone suggests that your class should perform *Titus Andronicus.*
a) Do you think that this would be a good idea? Why/Why not?
b) The person in charge of the English Department decides that she will not allow the students to perform the play. Look at the reasons for her decision and then try to find reasons for performing the play:
   i) a very early play/not one of Shakespeare's best plays
   ii) subject matter not appropriate - about Romans and Goths
   iii) much too violent - could disturb the minds of young people
   iv) very immoral - the good people don't seem to win
   v) not a very well-known play
   vi) there are many other plays to choose from.
c) Have a class debate and vote on whether the play should be performed or not.

Titus Andronicus is one of the most violent, bloody and cruel plays ever written! It is a real horror story! If someone made a realistic film of it today, many of the scenes would be so disgusting that no cinema would be allowed to show it. In this play many people are murdered; a young woman is raped and has her hands cut off and her tongue cut out so that she cannot identify her attackers; a father kills his daughter; a mother is tricked into eating a pie which contains her own children; a man is buried up to his neck and starved to death. Some of the worst scenes take place in a forest and here we can see that Shakespeare is describing something which he knows well – after all, Stratford was a town of only 2,000 inhabitants, surrounded by wooded countryside.

Here is Aaron, the most evil character in the play, giving his two sons advice about where to murder and rape:

The forest walks are wide and spacious;
And many unfrequented plots there are
Fitted by kind for rape and villainy...
The palace full of tongues, of eyes, and ears:
The woods are ruthless, dreadful, deaf, and dull;
There speak, and strike, brave boys, and take your turns;
There serve your lusts, shadow'd from heaven's eye...

(Act II, Scene I)

We see Aaron's truly evil nature when, at the end of the play, he says that he is sorry if he ever did a good deed:

If one good deed in all my life I did,
I do repent it from my very soul.

(Act V, Scene III)

For an audience who had recently lived through an attempted invasion and for whom death was an everyday occurrence, a play of this kind would have been very exciting. Indeed, most of the plays being written at this time were very violent.

5. PATRIOTS AND HISTORY PLAYS

A patriot is someone who is true to his ruler and his country. It was not difficult for ordinary people living at the time of Elizabeth I to be patriotic because England seemed to be doing very well. As we shall see, there were problems, the main one being religion, but it is true to say that Shakespeare grew up in a very patriotic society. In the 15th century, however, things were very different. This was not a happy time in English history – France eventually won the Hundred Years' War and pushed the English out of all French territory, but, worse still, there had been a terrible civil war in England, the Wars of the Roses, which were fought between the two greatest families of England – the Houses of York (the white rose) and Lancaster (the red rose). Although these wars had ended in 1485 with the defeat of the House of York at Bosworth, they were still part of the consciousness of the people. As a young dramatist writing 100 years later, Shakespeare did what writers throughout the ages have done – he began writing about the recent history of his own country. The first history plays that he wrote were *Henry VI Parts I, II & III* (1591/93) and, later on, *Richard III*.

Henry VI Part I deals with the war against the French and, in particular, with the part played by Joan of Arc. It is interesting to see Shakespeare dealing with a character who is obviously meant to be evil (because she is French and anti-English!) but, at the same time, very brave. Joan is the first in a long line of Shakespearian villains who are allowed to speak wonderful lines of poetry. Her last speech, when she curses the English, is a good example:

> *Then lead me hence; With whom I leave my curse.*
> *May never glorious sun reflex his beams*
> *Upon the country where you make abode,*
> *But darkness and the gloomy shade of death*
> *Environ you, till mischief and despair*
> *Drive you to break your necks or hang yourselves!*
>
> *(Act V, Scene VI)*

Just as when we watch a horror film and see a knife shining in the moonlight and know that something terrible is going to happen, so must Shakespeare's audience have felt a shiver of fear when they heard these lines. Joan of Arc is looking into the future and predicting the darkness and gloomy shade of death which was to be the Wars of the Roses. And just as a good film director

9

lets the audience see the knife before it is used, in order to build up the suspense and excitement, Shakespeare prepares his audience for the terrible fighting to come. Very early on in this play, in a famous scene (Act II, Scene IV), the nobles of England are shown in a garden, each one picking either a white or a red rose. The preparations are being made for civil war. By the last act of *Henry VI Part II,* civil war has broken out. The most interesting thing about these three plays is that they introduce one of Shakespare's great themes – the nature of kingship – and the first of Shakespeare's great tragic figures – Richard III.

We shall look at Shakespeare's idea of kingship later but we cannot leave our discussion of *Henry VI Part III* without seeing why Richard is such a great tragic figure. In this **soliloquy** from Act III, Scene II, he opens his heart to the audience and lets them see his real feelings. Because the image he uses – that of a child on his way home who is lost in a wood and is getting cut by all the thorns – is a very simple one, we feel sorry for him:

> *And yet I know not how to get the crown;*
> *For many lives stand between me and home.*
> *And I – like one lost in a thorny wood,*
> *That rends the thorns and is rent with the thorns,*
> *Seeking a way and straying from the way,*
> *Not knowing how to find the open air,*
> *But toiling desperately to find it out...*

But we must beware. This is not a sweet child who is lost; this is a monster:

> *Why, I can smile, and murder while I smile...*
> *And wet my cheeks with artificial tears,*
> *And frame my face to all occasions.*

By the end of the play, he is waiting like a spider, ready to strike.

6. RELIGION AND THE PURITANS

ACTIVITY:

The passage below, which describes the religious problem in Elizabethan England, is jumbled up. Rearrange the paragraphs to complete the text.

a) At this time there were many religious people in Europe protesting about the way the Catholic Church was organized under the Pope. These protesters, or Protestants as they became known, were obviously on the side of Henry and so the Church of England became Protestant and many English Catholics were persecuted.

b) It is interesting to see that Shakespeare didn't use religion as a theme in his plays although it was the single biggest problem in Elizabethan England. It was so important that Elizabeth passed a law in 1559 which prevented plays from discussing matters of religion!

c) The following declaration by a Puritan London preacher gives us some idea of the kind of people they were:
'The cause of plagues is sin, if you look to it well; and the cause of sin is plays; therefore the cause of plagues is plays'.

d) When Elizabeth I came to power she did not make the same mistake as Mary. Although she was Protestant, she did not cause too many problems for the English Catholics. Because the Protestants had suffered so much under Mary, during Elizabeth's reign many of them wanted to destroy anything that reminded them of Catholicism. They wanted England to be pure so they were called Puritans. Very soon they started attacking theatres as wicked, sinful places.

e) This would not have been such a problem if Henry's son, Edward VI, had lived longer. But he died and his place was taken by Henry's daughter Mary who was a Catholic and hated her father. She was responsible for killing so many Protestants in her five years as Queen that she became known as Bloody Mary.

f) The religious problem began when Elizabeth's father, Henry VIII, wanted to divorce his wife and marry again. He asked the Pope to grant him a divorce but the Pope refused. Henry then declared himself the head of the Christian Church in England and annulled his own marriage – that is, he declared that his marriage had been illegal.

DID YOU KNOW?
Henry VIII had six wives altogether, but not all at the same time!

There is a drink made of tomato juice and vodka which is called Bloody Mary because its red colour is the same as the colour of blood.

In five years, Mary I was responsible for almost 300 people being burnt alive because they were Protestant.

11

7. THE PLAGUE YEARS: 1592 – 1594

ACTIVITY:

The sentences in Column B can be matched with the sentences in Column A to form a complete text. Draw lines between them.

COLUMN A	COLUMN B
1. It is difficult for people nowadays to imagine what life was like almost 400 years ago.	A. There were two types of plague.
2. Families were very large and they lived all crammed together.	B. Only about three out of every ten people who were bitten by such fleas survived.
3. It was known as the Black Death because the bodies of its victims turned black.	C. There was no electricity, no gas, no water supply in your home, no toilet or bathroom.
4. One was spread when the patient coughed and filled the air with germs – pneumonic plague.	D. In these circumstances, disease was common and the worst disease of all was the plague or the Black Death.
5. The other form of plague, bubonic plague, was carried by a certain kind of insect – a flea – which lived on rats.	E. Normally, these fleas were not interested in other creatures but when they had the plague they started biting any flesh they could find.
6. There was no escape.	F. This type attacked the lungs and everyone who caught it died.

It is hardly possible to imagine what London must have been like during the plague. One writer described what it was like to walk through the streets at midnight: *Striking up alarm, servants crying for their masters, wives for husbands, parents for children, children for their mothers . . .* When the plague was discovered, men came along to shut up the house and the people who lived there were not allowed to leave for 28 days. So people used to hide the bodies of any family member who died, carry them out of the house at night and leave them to be found in the morning. Shakespeare would have known all about the plague because it was very common in Elizabethan England. However, in 1592, a new wave of the Black Death came to London and killed ten per cent of the population. All public meetings were stopped and, in June of that year, all the theatres were closed. They did not open again until May 1594. Shakespeare's life at this time is a mystery. Maybe he stayed in London. Maybe he went back home to Stratford. But one thing we do know – the plague years were very important for Shakespeare's development as a writer. Before the theatres closed, he was a popular dramatist, but certainly not the best: Christopher Marlowe and Thomas Kyd were better. By the end of 1594, both Marlowe and Kyd were dead. Shakespeare had become a principal member of a theatre company; he had written some great poetry and had made some powerful friends.

ACTIVITY:

1. Here is a children's nursery rhyme which dates from the time of the plague:
   Ring a ring of roses,
   A pocketful of posies.
   Atishoo! Atishoo!*
   We all fall down.
   (*Atishoo is the sound that people make when they sneeze.)
a) Why do you think people carried flowers around with them?
b) Which type of plague do you think is being described here?

2. Why do you think that people were shut up in their houses when it was discovered that one of their family had the plague?

II

THE ELIZABETHAN THEATRE

The Globe Theatre

1. DIFFERENCES

Think for a moment about going to 'he theatre. You arrange to meet a friend in the foyer at 7.45 p.r ι. for a play that begins at 8 p.m. The price of the ticket may oe quite high if you are going to see a popular play. If the play is successful, it may run for several months. The building is modern and well-designed, with air-conditioning, good lighting and very comfortable seats. You and your friend sit down, the lights go down slowly and the audience becomes very quiet. The play has begun . . .

If we are going to try to understand Shakespeare's plays we have to get rid of this picture completely because Elizabethan theatre was nothing like this at all! First of all, we must understand that plays and theatres were very new. The first English dramas were based on The Bible and developed into Morality Plays, which tried to teach people how to behave as well as entertain them. But in 16th-century London, the growing population wanted entertainment and, to meet that demand, professional theatres were established.

ACTIVITY:

Here are some statements about Elizabethan theatre. Working with a partner, try to guess which are true and which are false. Circle your choice.

a) The first theatre was called The Theatre.	T/F
b) Theatres were also called public houses.	T/F
c) Plays were put on at night.	T/F
d) Only men performed in plays.	T/F
e) Elizabethan theatres had the same design as theatres today.	T/F
f) Theatres were quite small and could hold only a few hundred people.	T/F
g) A lot of scenery was used to make the play more realistic.	T/F
h) Only rich people went to plays.	T/F

Now check your answers by reading quickly through the text below.

The first theatre, or playhouse, was built in 1576 by James Burbage. It was simply called The Theatre and was very successful. Soon other people started their own theatres to satisfy the growing demand for more and more plays.

These were performed in the afternoon by men and boys only. Women never took part and this may explain why so many of Shakespeare's plays present young men dressing up as women.

Male actors dressed as women

DID YOU KNOW?

Most of Shakespeare's plays were performed only once or twice, but the play *The Mousetrap*, a murder mystery written by Agatha Christie, has been running in London since 1952 and has been performed more than 100,000 times.

At the first performance of *Tamburlaine the Great* by Christopher Marlowe, the play needed the sound of battle and gunfire. Unfortunately, the gun went off in the wrong direction and a boy and a pregnant woman were killed.

Most of the theatres which were built were very large and could hold several thousand people. All sorts of people, rich and poor, came to see the plays. The people who paid the lowest price didn't even get a seat – they had to stand. Because they stood on the ground, they were called groundlings. Some people sat on the stage itself while others sat in galleries around and above the stage. The main stage was usually bare. The audience had to imagine the scene by listening to the language of the actors, which was very descriptive. Sometimes the scenery was only a written notice: THIS IS A HOUSE or THIS IS A FOREST .

Try to imagine what the theatre was like when Shakespeare was alive...

It is 4 o'clock in the afternoon. People have finished their work for the day. They want some entertainment and so they come to see Master Shakespeare's new play. Some people have been drinking and they are laughing loudly or quarrelling with their neighbours. Some are eating. Some are shouting to their friends in another part of the theatre. Many people are following the latest fashion and smoking tobacco. There are different smells and noises everywhere. Everyone is excited. There are thieves trying to steal money. There are prostitutes trying to find customers. There are beggars crying out for money and young babies crying for food. The groundlings have been standing waiting and now some of them are getting restless and they start to shout for the play to begin. Some of them may be so impatient that they have started throwing pieces of fruit or nut-shells! Suddenly there is the sound of a trumpet and the beating of a drum – the play has begun! The audience settles down to watch it. The actors on the stage are describing a battle – some old soldiers in the audience begin to cheer and someone else tells them to be quiet. The young men sitting on the stage start laughing and making rude comments. Some people become angry and shout at them. All this time the play is going on!

Inside a typical Elizabethan theatre

TALKING POINT:

The picture of a theatre on page 17 is very different from a theatre today. Try to identify as many differences as you can. Which do you prefer? Why?

In the time of Shakespeare, there was a great deal of drunkenness. English people had no tea or coffee and so they drank a lot of beer, which they called *mad dog, angels' food, dragons' milk, lift leg* and other such names. Can you explain each of these names? E.g. Beer was called mad dog because it made...

ACTIVITY:

Imagine that you are an Elizabethan Puritan. James Burbage is planning to build a theatre near your home.
a) What is your reaction?
b) What arguments can you make to the City Council to prevent the theatre from being built?

2. THE GLOBE THEATRE

ACTIVITY:

Read the following text and fill in each blank with one word from the box below.

to	where	had	who	so	with	the	with	to
new	secretly	down	very	was	already	in

James Burbage, _____ built the first theatre in London in 1576, died in 1597 while he was _____ the middle of business discussions _____ the landlord. Because Burbage's theatre _____ making so much money, the landlord wanted to increase the rent of the land _____ the theatre stood. After failing _____ come to an agreement _____ Burbage's family, the landlord decided to pull the theatre down and sell the wood. On _____ night of the 28th December, 1598, the two sons of James Burbage, Richard and Cuthbert, _____ arranged for some workmen to take _____ the theatre that their father _____ built and transport it across the River Thames to a _____ site on the south bank of the river. The new theatre which they built there was called The Globe. This whole operation cost money and a new company was formed _____ raise the necessary capital. Shakespeare took a tenth share. He was _____ wealthy because, using his good business instincts, he had bought a share in a previous company and _____ did not have to rely on the small amount of money he earned from writing and acting in plays.

TALKING POINT:

Some people say that it is impossible for a person to be a great writer and very rich at the same time.

Why do you think they say this? Do you agree? What about the great writers from your own country – are they rich or poor?

The Globe Theatre

3. SPIES AND MURDERERS

It is important to remember just how different Shakespeare was from the other great dramatists of the time. Christopher Marlowe, who was born in the same year as Shakespeare, 1564, developed his writing ability much faster. His first great play, *Tamburlaine the Great*, was produced in 1587 and after that he wrote five plays in very quick succession: *Dr Faustus, The Jew of Malta, Edward II, The Massacre at Paris* and *Dido, Queen of Carthage*.

He died at the early age of 29 in very mysterious circumstances – stabbed to death by his companion in a fight in a tavern. The fight was said to have been about who was going to pay the bill. Although Marlowe was a violent man who had previously been charged with attacking someone with a knife, it is very likely that he was murdered because he was involved in spying against powerful Catholic nobles.

Certainly his friend and fellow writer, Thomas Kyd, was involved in some secret plot. The two men shared the same lodgings and, when certain papers were found in their room, Kyd was tortured on the rack and confessed.

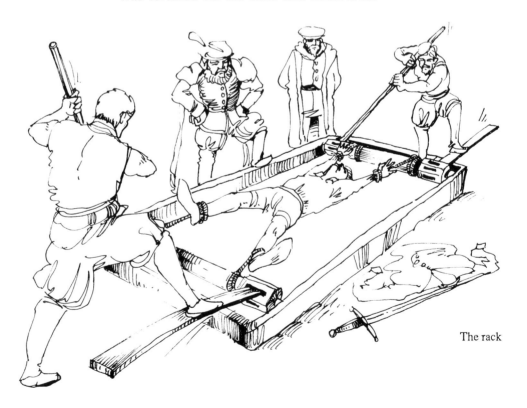

The rack

Kyd's great revenge play, *The Spanish Tragedy*, first performed in 1587 or 1588, had a great influence on Shakespeare's early writing and it is clear that *Titus Andronicus*, for example, is his attempt to copy what Kyd was doing. After having been tortured, Kyd was a broken man physically and mentally and he died, in poverty and disgrace, in 1594.

If both of these great dramatists had not died, it is interesting to speculate whether Shakespeare would have been as famous as he is today. Certainly, if Shakespeare had died at the same time as Marlowe, it is Marlowe who would be remembered as the greater writer. Shakespeare needed a few more years before he began to produce his best work.

Another contemporary of Shakespeare's and one of his best friends, was the playwright Ben Jonson (1572-1637). During his career, Jonson was imprisoned several times for attacking the Government through his writing, convicted of killing a man and was almost certainly a government spy as Marlowe had been before him.

TALKING POINT:
Why do you think writers such as Marlowe and Jonson might have made good spies? What kind of people would make good spies today?

Shakespeare seems to have stayed away from all types of conflict, personal or political. He doesn't seem to have fought any duels, spied on his colleagues, been involved in drunken fights in taverns, been thrown into prison or done any of the other things typical of Elizabethan gentlemen. In this way he was very different from his friends and fellow writers – not a very Elizabethan man at all, in fact!

ACTIVITY:
Imagine that one of the best-known writers in your country is involved in a murder. Try to make up the story that would appear in the newspaper. What would the headline be? What would other people say about it?

4. A PLAYER'S THEATRE

If we look at the world of drama today, we will see that the person with the most influence is not the writer or the actor, but the director. People nowadays discuss different versions of a Shakespearean play, for example, by identifying who the director was.

In Shakespeare's day, however, things were very different. One of the most important guarantees of a play's success was the principal actor. An actor had to know the skills of juggling, acrobatics, fencing, dancing, and so on. Shakespeare's long-time friend and business partner, Richard Burbage, was possibly the best actor of the time and it is clear that many Shakespearean roles such as Shylock in *The Merchant of Venice*, and Hamlet, were written with him in mind. Most critics now agree, in fact, that Shakespeare often wrote parts for Burbage and others which allowed them to show off their skills to the audience.

Clowns were another great favourite with the crowds although not always with the dramatist himself. Actors playing clown roles would often omit some of their lines, invent dialogue of their own or tell jokes which they had recently heard. The greatest clown of the Elizabethan age was Will Kempe. He was a brilliant clown and Shakespeare was not the only dramatist who complained about Kempe's independence – Ben Jonson complained because Kempe sometimes left out his lines altogether and started joking with members of the audience.

DID YOU KNOW?
Will Kempe danced all the way from the city of London to the city of Norwich. It took him nine days and he wrote a very successful book about it. Later he tried to dance to Rome but he wasn't successful.

Will Kempe

The clown served several functions in Shakespeare's plays: he provided the audience with some fun after the dramatic action; he gave the audience, musicians and actors a chance to rest and he also gave the actors a chance to change costumes if necessary. Most importantly, the clown provided an alternative, common-sense view of the action of the play.

In *The Merchant of Venice,* for example, the clown Launcelot Gobbo meets his father by accident on the street. His father is blind and doesn't know who he is talking to. Launcelot decides to *'try confusions with him'* - i.e. he is going to try to confuse his old blind father.

> Old Gobbo: *Master young gentleman, you, I pray you, which is the way to master Jew's?*
> Launcelot: *Turn up on your right hand at the next turning, but, at the next turning of all, on your left, marry at the very next turning, turn of no hand, but turn down indirectly to the Jew's house.*
> Old Gobbo: *By God's sonties, 'twill be a hard way to hit.*
> (Act II, Scene II)

TALKING POINT:
Do you find it funny that a son would tease his old blind father by giving him confusing directions? Why?/Why not?

Now this is very simple humour and would have been very funny to the people of London. Like Shakespeare himself, many of them had come to the big city from the country. In their first few months they must sometimes have found themselves lost amid all the houses and streets of the fast-growing city.

It is typical of Shakespeare to show us the parallel action of two children deceiving their parents in two very different ways. Launcelot is only playing with his father in fun – he tells him who he is immediately afterwards, but, as with a lot of the clowning in Shakespeare's plays, there is another side to it – a more serious side. Launcelot works for Shylock, the master Jew, and his daughter Jessica, who, with Launcelot's help, deceives her father and runs away to be married to Lorenzo, taking money and jewels with her. Jessica's action is partly responsible for her father's downfall.

ACTIVITY:
Try to find three things that everyone in your class finds funny. Try to say what makes these things funny. Is there any difference between what men and women find funny?

III

THE LANGUAGE OF SHAKESPEARE

> *'There is a tide in the affairs of men*
> *Which, taken at the flood, leads on to fortune;*
> *Omitted, all the voyage of their life*
> *Is bound in shallows and in miseries.*
> *On such a full sea are we now afloat.'*

Julius Caesar (Act IV, Sc III)

1. THE RISING TIDE

As we have learnt, in 1592 the theatres closed because of the plague. From this time, until 1600, Shakespeare produced a series of plays which include most of his best comedies. Some writers look back over his career and describe the plays he wrote during this period as immature. To a certain extent this is true but we must remember that they are not immature compared to the work of other dramatists – they are only immature when we compare them with his other plays.

Here is a list of the plays that Shakespeare wrote, from *Titus Andronicus* in 1589/90 to *The Merry Wives of Windsor* in 1600, in the approximate order in which they were written:

Titus Andronicus
Henry VI, Parts I, II, III
The Taming of the Shrew
The Comedy of Errors
Love's Labour's Lost
The Two Gentlemen of Verona
Richard III
A Midsummer Night's Dream
Romeo and Juliet
Richard II
King John
The Merchant of Venice
Henry IV, Parts I & II
Much Ado About Nothing
Henry V
Julius Caesar
As You Like It
The Merry Wives of Windsor

During this same period he also wrote a series of poems. (We shall look at some of these later.) If we remember that, in addition to all of this, he was still a principal actor who had to learn his lines and rehearse his parts, not only in plays written by himself but in other people's plays as well, we can see that he must have been a very hardworking writer, determined to be successful.

ACTIVITY:

1. Here is a list of adjectives which can describe a person's attitude to work. Working with a partner, arrange them into two categories: positive (P) or negative (N). Circle your choice.

efficient P/N	lazy P/N	enthusiastic P/N
indolent P/N	complacent P/N	unreceptive P/N
eager P/N	industrious P/N	dynamic P/N
thorough P/N	lackadaisical P/N	painstaking P/N

*Now decide which adjectives describe **YOUR** attitude to work. **BE HONEST!***

2. Some nationalities have a reputation for being hard-working. Working in groups, decide who you think are the most hard-working nationalities. Number them 1 - 11.

Russian	_____
American	_____
Chinese	_____
British	_____
Japanese	_____
Indian	_____
German	_____
Vietnamese	_____
Swiss	_____
Kenyan	_____
Taiwanese	_____

Do the other groups agree? What reasons do you have for your opinion?

The title of this section is *The Rising Tide* and it is intended to suggest a period in which Shakespeare was becoming better and better at writing but not yet at his peak. By comparing Shakespeare's progress to a tide of the sea which rises until it is full, we are using an **image**. The two most common types of images are **metaphors** and **similes**.

We use a metaphor when we compare two things by saying one thing is something else. For example, when Romeo is hiding in Juliet's garden, she comes to the window and she is so beautiful that when Romeo sees her, he says:

But, soft! what light through yonder window breaks?
It is the east, and Juliet is the sun.

(Act II, Scene II)

We use a simile when we compare two things by saying one thing is similar to something else – for example in *Julius Caesar,* Caesar is asked to change his mind about something but he refuses, saying:

as sober as a judge
as drunk as a lord

I am constant as the northern star.

(Act III, Scene I)

Images are more often used in poetry than in prose. Shakespeare is a great dramatic poet and uses unforgettable imagery.

ACTIVITY:
Here are three extracts from Shakespeare's plays of this period which show the beauty of his imagery. As you read through each one, try to identify the image and say if it is a metaphor or a simile. (Don't worry if you can't understand every word.)

a) *All the world's a stage,*
And all the men and women merely players.
They have their exits and their entrances,
And one man in his time plays many parts
As You Like It *(Act II, Scene VII)*

b) *The quality of mercy is not strained.*
It droppeth as the gentle rain from heaven
Upon the place beneath. It is twice blesst:
It blesseth him that gives, and him that takes
The Merchant of Venice *(Act IV, Scene I)*

c) *Then let me go, and hinder not my course:*
I'll be as patient as a gentle stream
The Two Gentlemen of Verona *(Act II, Scene VII)*

However, Shakespeare's dramatic poetry is not only about beauty. Some of his most powerful speeches concern violence, betrayal, war and death.

ACTIVITY:

Here are three more extracts. Try to do the same as you did with the three previous extracts.

> d) *No more the thirsty entrance of this soil*
>   *Shall daub her lips with her own children's blood*
>   Henry IV, Part I *(Act I, Scene I)*

> e) *From forth the kennel of thy womb hath crept*
>   *A hell-hound that doth hunt us all to death*
>   Richard III *(Act IV, Scene IV)*

> f) *Thou cold-blooded slave,*
>   *Hast thou not spoke like thunder on my side?*
>   King John *(Act III, Scene I)*

ACTIVITY:

Richard III is described as 'a hell-hound' – a dog from hell. People can often be compared to animals. Someone who eats in a greedy way can be called a pig and someone who behaves in a dishonest or nasty way can be called a rat!

Here are some expressions but they are jumbled up. Match the adjectives in column A with the animals in column B.

A	B
1. As wise as	a) an ox.
2. As stubborn as	b) a lion.
3. As brave as	c) an owl.
4. As dead as	d) a wolf.
5. As cunning as	e) an elephant.
6. As strong as	f) a mouse.
7. As quiet as	g) a donkey.
8. As blind as	h) a fox.
9. As large as	i) a dodo.
10. As hungry as	j) a bat.

TALKING POINT:
Look at the descriptions in the previous activity. In your culture, do you use the same animals to describe people in the same way? What are the differences, if any? Can you explain these differences?

2. A COMPARISON

By 1600, Shakespeare was half-way through his writing career. His last play, *The Tempest,* would be written in 1612/1613. In the dozen or so years that he had been writing for the stage he had learnt a great deal – first by copying the style of Marlowe and Kyd, and then by experimenting with new styles that he invented. In order to see how Shakespeare's language developed over these first 12 years, we will look at two short speeches, one from an early play, *Titus Andronicus* and one from a later play, *Julius Caesar.* These plays are similar in that they are both set in Rome, they both deal with murder and revenge and they both explore the pain of suffering. But there the similarities end.

We have already seen how Shakespere's audience demanded entertainment more than anything else and that a successful dramatist had to give his characters thrilling speeches which would satisfy restless Elizabethan audiences.

Here is the first of the two speeches, both of which are filled with horror. Aaron is asked if he is sorry for all the evil that he has done:

Lucius: *Art thou not sorry for these heinous deeds?*
Aaron: *Ay, that I had not done a thousand more.*
Even now I curse the day – and yet I think
Few come within the compass of my curse –
Wherein I did not some notorious ill,
As kill a man, or else devise his death,
Ravish a maid, or plot the way to do it;
Accuse some innocent, and foreswear myself;
Set deadly enmity between two friends;
Make poor men's cattle break their necks;
Set fire on barns and haystacks in the night,
And bid the owners quench them with their tears.
Oft have I digged up dead men from their graves
And set them upright at their dear friends' door,
Even when their sorrows almost was forgot,
And on their skins, as on the bark of trees,
Have with my knife carved in Roman letters,
'Let not your sorrow die, though I am dead'.
But! I have done a thousand dreadful things
As willingly as one would kill a fly,
And nothing grieves me heartily indeed
But that I cannot do ten thousand more.

Titus Andronicus *(Act V, Scene I)*

'Oft have I digged up dead men from their graves'

Titus Andronicus (Act V, Sc I)

Aaron is being presented here as an evil monster but notice that most of the evil deeds he describes are the kind of things that would not have been too unusual in Shakespeare's time, particularly in the countryside around Stratford. The dramatic effect is achieved through Aaron listing all the evil he has done and regretting that he cannot do more. The language is plain and effective but it does not have the power to thrill us, to make us really afraid. One very typical Shakespearean 'double' image here is when Aaron describes the farmers trying to *'quench'* (put out) the fires *'with their tears'*. These tears have two causes: the smoke and seeing their hard-earned produce go up in smoke!

If we compare Aaron's speech to the one that Mark Antony makes over the body of his murdered friend, Julius Caesar, we will see that Shakespeare's language has become much more poetic and powerful:

> *O pardon me, thou bleeding piece of earth,*
> *That I am meek and gentle with these butchers.*
> *Thou art the ruins of the noblest man*
> *That ever lived in the tide of times.*
> *Woe to the hand that shed this costly blood!*
> *Over thy wounds now do I prophesy —*
> *Which like dumb mouths do ope their ruby lips.*
> *To beg the voice and utterance of my tongue —*
> *A curse shall light upon the limbs of men;*

Domestic fury and fierce civil strife
Shall cumber all the parts of Italy;
Blood and destruction shall be so in use,
And dreadful objects so familiar,
That mothers shall but smile when they behold
Their infants quarter'd with the hands of war,
All pity chok'd with custom of fell deeds;
And Caesar's spirit, ranging for revenge,
With Ate by his side come hot from hell,
Shall in these confines with a monarch's voice
Cry 'havoc!' and let slip the dogs of war,
That this foul deed shall smell above the earth
With carrion men, groaning for burial.

Julius Caesar *(Act III, Scene I)*

TALKING POINT:
Read again the list of Aaron's crimes. Which one do you think is the worst? Why? Do you think that people should be put to death if they commit terrible crimes? In groups, try to find as many arguments as possible for both viewpoints and have a debate.

This speech is full of powerful images. Caesar's body is described as *'a bleeding piece of earth'*, his wounds are *'dumb mouths'*, and so on.

Ate was the Greek goddess of mischief and reckless actions, so Mark Antony is saying that Caesar's murder was reckless and that he requires revenge. Shakespeare doesn't have to make a list of horrors as he did in *Titus Andronicus* – the single image of mothers who only smile as their babies are butchered in front of them is enough to show us what true horror is.

But notice that Shakespeare's language has not become more complicated - *'hot from hell'*, *'the dogs of war'*, *'this foul deed shall smell above the earth'*; this is very simple language but very effective.

ACTIVITY:
Working in groups, try to summarize in 100 words what Antony prophesies.
('A curse shall light upon...' etc.)

3. SHAKESPEARE'S POETRY

We have looked at Shakespeare's language, in particular his use of images, but you may be wondering why he is described as a poet. After all, there are no **rhymes** in the two speeches we looked at on pages 30 and 31.

Look at this short extract from *The Merchant of Venice*. Jessica is making plans to deceive her father, Shylock, and run away with Lorenzo, whom she loves:

Alack, what heinous sin is it in me
To be asham'd to be my father's child!
But though I am a daughter to his blood,
I am not to his manners. O Lorenzo,
If thou keep promise I shall end this strife,
Become a Christian and thy loving wife.

(Act II, Scene III)

'I gave my love a ring and made him swear
Never to part with it; and here he stands'
The Merchant of Venice
(Act V, Sc I)

The first thing to notice is that the last two lines rhyme: *'strife/wife'*. This is called a **rhyming couplet** and was usually used to end a scene.

Shakespeare also wrote whole speeches in rhyme. The short speech below is from *Romeo and Juliet*. Here, Romeo is trying to describe how beautiful Juliet is as she dances.

This is *very* romantic – true love at first sight!

O, She doth teach the torches to burn bright!
It seems she hangs upon the cheek of night
As a rich jewel in an Ethiope's ear –
Beauty too rich for use, for earth too dear!
So shows a snowy dove trooping with crows
As yonder lady o'er her fellows shows.
The measure done, I'll watch her place of stand,
And, touching hers, make blessed my rude hand.
Did my heart love till now? Forswear it, sight!
For I ne'er saw true beauty till this night.

(Act I, Scene V)

'*...but this I pray, That thou consent to marry us today*'
Romeo and Juliet (Act II, Sc III)

But poetry is not simply rhyme – there must be **rhythm** too. You may not have noticed but all of the extracts you have read so far have had the same rhythm. To discover this for yourself, count the number of **syllables** in the following lines:

QUESTION:
How many syllables are
there in each line?

It seems she hangs upon the cheek of night
Romeo and Juliet *(Act I, Scene V)*
O pardon me, thou bleeding piece of earth
Julius Caesar *(Act III, Scene I)*
If thou keep promise, I shall end this strife
The Merchant of Venice *(Act II, Scene III)*
Set fire on barns and haystacks in the night
Titus Andromicus *(Act V, Scene I)*

Shakespeare wrote two kinds of poetry. The first uses rhyming couplets and the second uses **blank verse**. This is poetry which does not rhyme but which still has a very regular rhythm: each line has ten syllables and there is a fixed **stress** pattern, the first syllable being weak and the second strong.

It 'seems she 'hangs u'pon the 'cheek of 'night

O 'pardon 'me, thou 'bleeding 'piece of 'earth

If 'thou keep 'promise, 'I shall 'end this 'strife

Set 'fire on 'barns and 'haystacks 'in the 'night

In English, this kind of line is called an **iambic pentameter**.
iambic = 2 syllables, one weak followed by one strong
pentameter = 5 pairs of syllables

Now you should be able to see why Shakespeare sometimes shortens a word like *over* into *o'ver*, or *never* into *ne'er*. It is because he needs a word of only one syllable to fit into the line.
Another common feature, which you may already have noticed, is that he sometimes writes the past verb forms in full, e.g.

That ever lived in the tide of times

but sometimes he shortens them, e.g.

All pity chok'd with custom of fell deeds

If you count the syllables and then say the lines aloud, you should notice that *'lived'* should be pronounced as two syllables, with the stress on the first:

That 'ever 'lived 'in the 'tide of 'times

but that *'chok'd'* should be pronounced as one syllable:

All 'pity 'chok'd with 'custom 'of fell 'deeds

However, Shakespeare did not simply follow a formula for writing which meant that each line had ten syllables, that every second syllable was stressed and that sometimes the last words of each pair of lines should rhyme. This would have been very boring! Shakespeare changed and developed and, as we shall see, created entirely new kinds of dramatic poetry.

ACTIVITY:
Here again is Mark Antony's speech over the body of Caesar. Read each line slowly, several times and then mark the syllables which are stressed. Remember that there may be some lines which do not follow the pattern we have looked at. These make the verse more interesting to listen to.

O pardon me, thou bleeding piece of earth,
That I am meek and gentle with these butchers,
Thou art the ruins of the noblest man
That ever lived in the tide of times.
Woe to the hand that shed this costly blood!
Over thy wounds now do I prophesy –
Which like dumb mouths do ope their ruby lips,
To beg the voice and utterance of my tongue
A curse shall light upon the limbs of men;
Domestic fury and fierce civil strife
Shall cumber all the parts of Italy;
Blood and destruction shall be so in use,
And dreadful objects so familiar,
That mothers shall but smile when they behold
Their infants quarter'd with the hands of war,
All pity chok'd with custom of fell deeds:
And Caesar's spirit, ranging for revenge,
With Ate by his side come hot from hell,
Shall in these confines with a monarch's voice
Cry 'havoc!' and let slip the dogs of war,
That this foul deed shall smell above the earth
With carrion men, groaning for burial.

4. WORDS, WORDS, WORDS

If we go to most countries in the world, we will find the English language. Words such as *telephone, hotel, taxi,* etc., have become part of the language of most people who live in or near a town in many parts of the world. English has become such an international language that it is difficult to understand what the English language was like in 16th-century England. Because England was on an island, it was quite separate from the rest of Europe. The language of the English people, therefore, had stayed the same for hundreds of years. From the middle of the 16th century, however, things began to change.

We saw in Chapter 1 that explorers and pirates were busy opening up the world for English traders, that the threat of a Spanish invasion disappeared with the destruction of the Armada and that England was enjoying peace and prosperity under Elizabeth. There was a feeling of growing excitement which Shakespeare and his companions must have been aware of – English society was changing and developing very rapidly, people were slowly moving from the countryside to the cities, more and more books were being written and printed in English, knowledge was spreading, the theatre was becoming more and more popular. Shakespeare and the other dramatists of the age desperately needed more and more words in order to write their plays and keep their audiences happy, but the number of words available to them was limited. What could they do?

The answer was simple – they would take them from other sources. Just as pirates like Drake and Hawkins were stealing gold and silver from the Spanish, Elizabethan dramatists stole words. They took them from other parts of Britain, where people used many **dialect** words not known in London; from the sailors who returned home from other lands; from Portuguese and Spanish; from the Far East and West; from French; from Greek and, most of all, from Latin. In the 45 years of Elizabeth's reign, from 1558 to 1603, the English language changed more than it ever has since.

DID YOU KNOW?
The English language contains about 490,000 words (not counting all scientific and technical terms) and the average educated native English speaker has an oral vocabulary of about 5,000 words and a written vocabulary of about 10,000 words. Shakespeare, who never went to university, had a vocabulary of 15,000 words!

THE LANGUAGE OF SHAKESPEARE

TALKING POINT:

In groups, try to identify ten English words which are commonly used in your own language. Compare your list of words to those of the other groups. How many are there altogether? Do all of these words have something in common? Do you think that it is a good thing or a bad thing for your language to 'borrow' words from English? Try to think of arguments for and against and then have a class debate.

COMPREHENSION:

Answer these questions on the text from section 4.

1. a) What is the main point of paragraph 1?
    i)   English is an international language.
    ii) England is on an island.
    iii) People can't understand why English became an international language.
    iv) Because English is an international language, people can't understand what it was like before.
    v)   The English language stayed the same for hundreds of years.

    b) What is the main point of paragraph 2?
    i)   Shakespeare and his companions felt excited.
    ii)   Explorers and pirates were opening up the world.
    iii) There were great changes in society.
    iv)   Dramatists felt the need for a bigger vocabulary.
    v)   People started moving from the countryside to the cities.

    c) What is the main point of paragraph 3?
    i)   Pirates stole silver and gold.
    ii)   The English language changed in the 16th century.
    iii) Dramatists were responsible for bringing many new words into the English language.
    iv)   The English Language changed slightly in Elizabethan times.
    v)   The English are thieves.

2. Which of the following words are originally English and which come from other languages?

> alcohol   judo   restaurant   telephone   rhyme
> poetry   professor   car   piano   lecturer

IV
SHAKESPEARE'S
DRAMATIC ACHIEVEMENT

'Here hung those lips that I have kissed
I know not how oft'

Hamlet (Act V, Sc I)

1. THE END OF AN AGE

ACTIVITY:
Read through the following passage quickly to find the answers to these questions:
a) What kind of play is The Merchant Of Venice?
b) What happened in 1485?
c) Is it true that Richard III was an evil king?
d) When did Elizabeth I die?

Up to 1600, Shakespeare had written several different types of play: history plays such as *Henry IV* and *Richard III*; comedies such as *A Midsummer Night's Dream* and *A Comedy of Errors*; one early tragedy – *Romeo and Juliet;* one Roman tragedy – *Julius Caesar,* and a play which doesn't fit neatly into any single category – *The Merchant of Venice.* When he was writing his history plays, Shakespeare had to be very careful to present recent history in a way which was acceptable to Queen Elizabeth I. King Richard III, as Shakespeare presents him, is a monster, *'A hell-hound that doth hunt us all to death',* but modern historians agree that this is not a true picture. Richard III was a practical, hard-working ruler. However, he was defeated in 1485 by Elizabeth's grandfather, Henry Tudor, who became Henry VII. We have seen how cautious and sensible a man Shakespeare was compared to his fellow dramatists, so it is not surprising that he presented Richard in a way that would please Elizabeth.

In 1600, however, Elizabeth I had only three more years to live. She was losing her firm grip on the state and things were beginning to go wrong for her. Many of her closest advisers were unhappy with the decisions she was making. Her most dangerous enemy was her favourite nobleman, the Earl of Essex, who had very powerful friends, including King James VI of Scotland. One of Essex's closest friends was Lord Southampton, the man who had given so much support to Shakespeare. Ordinary people could sense that there was revolution in the air and many critics have claimed that Shakespeare wrote the play *Julius Caesar* as a warning to Essex and Southampton, although there is no actual evidence for this view.

What is true, however, is that during this very troubled period in Elizabeth's reign, Shakespeare wrote a play which tells the story of a highly intelligent man who is faced with a very difficult decision. This play was *Hamlet* – probably the best-known of all Shakespeare's plays.

2. HAMLET, PRINCE OF DENMARK

The opening scene of the play takes place at night on the walls of a castle, where a soldier, Francisco, is on guard. It is very cold so he has wrapped his cloak around himself. Suddenly, there is a shout:

Bernardo: *Who's there?*
Francisco: *Nay, answer me. Stand and unfold yourself.*
Bernardo: *Long live the King!*
Francisco: *Bernardo?*
Bernardo: *He.*

Now, this is very strange. Francisco is on duty and Bernardo has come to relieve him because it is now Bernardo's turn. It should be Francisco who speaks first, to find out who this newcomer is. There is obviously something strange happening because even when Bernardo gives the password (the secret word(s) which tell soldiers that they are fighting for the same side – *'Long live the King!'*), Francisco is still not sure who this person is. He thinks it's Bernardo but he is not certain, so he turns the name into a question – *'Bernardo?'*. It is only when Bernardo replies that the two soldiers are satisfied and start their conversation. Only fifteen words have been spoken so far but Shakespeare has already made us aware that there must be some reason why these two soldiers are acting so strangely and appear so frightened, even though they are in their own castle.

ACTIVITY:
Read the following dialogue:

A: *Excuse me! Oh, it's you.*
B: *Yes, it's me.*
A: *What are you doing here?*
B: *None of your business!*

Work with your partner and answer the following questions. Who do you think A and B are? Do they know each other well? What is their relationship? What kind of situation is this?

When you have done this, act out the dialogue and ask another pair of students to say who they think you are, where you are, etc.

Do the same with these two dialogues:

> A: Yes?
> B: Nothing.
> A: What do you mean 'Nothing'?
> B: It's all right. I'm sorry to have bothered you.

> A: I'm sorry.
> B: Are you?
> A: Yes. I won't do it again.
> B: No. You won't.

Now try to write three similar dialogues.

We quickly discover the reason for the strange behaviour of Francisco and Bernardo. They have twice seen a ghost walking along the walls of the castle – a ghost who looks exactly like the old king who has just died, Hamlet's father. Hamlet's friend, Horatio, sees the ghost too and decides that he will ask Hamlet to come and see it. This is a very exciting beginning to a play – fear, mystery and a ghost – just what Elizabethan audiences enjoyed! In Scene II we meet Hamlet. The first words he says are directed not at any of the characters in the play but at us, the audience. We realize that he is somehow separate from the other characters in the drama and from everything that is going on. In some way, he stands between the audience and the action of the play. The next thing he does is to distinguish between appearance and reality when he says to his mother:

> *Seems, madam? Nay, it* is. *I know not 'seems'.*
> *(Act I, Scene II)*

Just as Francisco is not sure about the identity of the person who disturbs him on the castle walls – it 'seems' to be Barnardo but he is not sure – so Hamlet is telling us to be careful. In this castle there is a great difference between 'seems' and 'is', between appearance and reality. In the play, Hamlet, the young prince of Denmark, acts rather like a tourist guide, with the audience as the tourists. Hamlet leads us around the castle, the centre of government, pointing out the many differences here between truth and illusion. He does this in a series of powerful speeches or soliloquies, where he is talking to himself. However, he is also talking to us, his audience.

'I am thy father's spirit,
Doomed for a certain time to
walk the night,
And for the day confined to
fast in fires'

Hamlet (Act I, Sc V)

By the end of Act I we have discovered that the ghost is that of Hamlet's father, the old king. He tells Hamlet that he was murdered by his brother, who then married his widow, Hamlet's mother. The ghost demands that Hamlet should take revenge by punishing his evil brother who is now the king.

This type of action was commonly found in **revenge tragedies** which were very popular with Elizabethan audiences. In fact, the story of *Hamlet* had already been made into a play before Shakespeare adapted it. The audience would have known, then, what Hamlet's next move was going to be. He has to 'hide' his true feelings from everyone, because, if the king suspected that Hamlet had discovered the truth, he would arrange to have him murdered. Hamlet forces his friends to swear that they will say nothing about the ghost and that they will not say anything if they discover him acting strangely.

The rest of the play is, on one level, simply the acting out of the ghost's demand for revenge, and, like all revenge tragedies, *Hamlet* ends with almost all the main characters dead: Hamlet; Gertrude, his mother; Claudius, his father's murderer; Polonius, the old counsellor; Polonius' daughter Ophelia, Hamlet's girl-friend, who commits suicide, and Polonius' son Laertes, who kills Hamlet in revenge for killing his father, Polonius. On this level, then, the play is very violent entertainment, full of ghosts, madness, poison, spies and murder.

43

TALKING POINT:
Suicide has become a problem affecting young people in many parts of the world. Is it a problem in your country? What are the reasons for it? Can anything be done about it?

TALKING POINT:
Do you think that all governments are as corrupt and dishonest as the one that Hamlet shows us? Why?/Why not?

DISCUSSION:
Do you believe in ghosts? Have you any experience of ghosts? Can you think of works of literature in your own language which seem to reflect the mood of the time in which they were written?

But it is also a very philosophical play. (One easy way of measuring Shakespeare's development as a dramatist is to compare his two revenge tragedies – *Titus Andronicus*, which is all horror and violent action, and *Hamlet*.) The audience is forced to think about the issues of appearance and reality, love and death, the duty of children towards their parents, the duty of a ruler to his country, the duty of a friend to a friend, and so on. Most of these problems are raised in Hamlet's soliloquies. For example, his famous soliloquy on whether or not he should commit suicide begins:

> *To be, or not to be; that is the question:*
> *Whether 'tis nobler in the mind to suffer*
> *The slings and arrows of outrageous fortune,*
> *Or to take arms against a sea of troubles,*
> *And, by opposing, end them? . . .*
>
> *(Act III, Scene I)*

It is surely significant that this dark, violent play, full of philosophical questioning, should have appeared when it did, when the government of Elizabeth I was very close to falling. Through the character of Hamlet, Shakespeare takes his audience on a guided tour through a kingdom of lies and hypocrisy, where people say things which they do not believe and where the truth is hidden.

Hamlet is probably the most popular of Shakespeare's plays. People have studied it and discussed it for hundreds of years and millions of words have been written about it. Most British schoolchildren are forced to read it and they usually have to learn some of Hamlet's soliloquies by heart.

One funny story may show you how much the play has affected the English language. In the 18th century, King George II went to see the play for the first time, but he didn't like it very much because, he said, it was full of quotations!

3. REBELLION AND KINGSHIP

We don't know if *Julius Caesar* and *Hamlet* were written as warnings to men like Essex and Southampton but, if they were, these men didn't pay any attention. Essex rebelled against Elizabeth but it was a very weak, badly organized attempt to overthrow the government. He was arrested, charged with treason, convicted and executed in February, 1601. Southampton was imprisoned, not to be released until after Elizabeth's death.

Robert, Earl of Essex

On the Saturday before Essex's rebellion, some of his friends persuaded Shakespeare's theatre company, the Chamberlain's Men, to put on a production of *Richard II*. This play tells the story of how a weak, uncertain king loses his throne to a more dynamic, practical person. Obviously, Essex's friends saw their hero getting rid of the old ruler, Elizabeth, and putting some life back into the government of the country. Shakespeare and his men were put into a very dangerous situation. If they performed, they would offend the queen; if they didn't, they would offend Essex and Southampton.

At first they refused, saying that the play was unfashionable, but they were then offered quite a large amount of money which they accepted. When Essex was captured, Shakespeare and the other players sent a representative to explain to the government what had happened. He was obviously effective because nothing happened to the Chamberlain's Men.

ROLEPLAY:
Imagine that you are a member of the Chamberlain's Men. Work in groups and try to act out the argument which they must have had before agreeing to put on *Richard II*.

DISCUSSION:
Do you think that Shakespeare was right not to directly criticize the bad things which he must have seen happening in the Government?

ACTIVITY:
As you read the following passage, fill in each blank with one of the words from the list below.

by	first	which	whether	rather	watching	could	
when	be	never	point	other	so	price	didn't	that

One theme _____ runs through Shakespeare's English history plays, *Julius Caesar,* his _____ Roman history tragedies like *Coriolanus* and *Antony and Cleopatra* and through *Hamlet* too, is the question of _____ it is right to get rid of a bad ruler. Kings (and queens!) were believed to _____ answerable only to God, and only God _____ get rid of them. Elizabeth I certainly supported _____ view and her successor, James VI of Scotland who became James I of England and Scotland, wrote a book explaining the idea of 'the divine right of kings'. The only problem was that Elizabeth's family, the Tudors, had gained the crown of England _____ rebelling! Shakespeare is _____ directly political. We cannot tell what view he supported but we must never forget the effect that _____ his plays must have had. Most of his audience could not read _____ they had only a very dim view of history. Shakespeare's plays, for them, must have had the same kind of effect as television _____ had on audiences in our century. Because they saw things, people believed them. One final _____ we should remember is that, by 1600, Shakespeare was working in a different kind of theatre – indoor _____ than outdoor. This meant that the scenery could be much better. It also meant a rise in the _____ of tickets so the very poor people (the 'groundlings') who had gone to Shakespeare's early plays probably _____ go to his later ones. One result was that he could make his plays more philosophical because he was writing for a richer, better-educated audience.

4. TWELFTH NIGHT

1 The period between 1600 and 1608 was the high tide of Shake-
2 speare's dramatic achievement, when he wrote his four great
3 tragedies, *Hamlet, Othello, Macbeth* and *King Lear*. His other
4 tragedies of this period are *Antony and Cleopatra, Coriolanus*
5 and *Timon of Athens*. The other plays he wrote at this time –
6 *Troilus and Cressida* and *Measure For Measure* – are very
7 difficult to classify, just as *The Merchant Of Venice* is also
8 difficult to classify. These two plays are concerned with
9 moral behaviour and, in particular, sexual behaviour and this
10 theme connects them very closely to *Hamlet*. There is not much
11 fun in either of these plays and we can see that Shakespeare's
12 mind must have been on much darker, more serious and tragic
13 matters. The two plays which are exceptions to this general
14 pattern of darkness, evil and death are *All's Well That Ends*
15 *Well* and *Twelfth Night*. The first of these is not a great play
16 and perhaps it was something that Shakespeare wrote very
17 quickly, for a special occasion. But *Twelfth Night* is a mas-
18 terpiece of comedy.

ACTIVITY:
*Read through the above paragraph again and identify what the following
pronouns refer to. The first one has been done for you as an example.*
a) line 2: he = Shakespeare
b) line 4: this
c) line 8: these
d) line 9: this
e) line 11: these
f) line 16: it

The plot of *Twelfth Night* is very difficult to summarize. It
deals with a brother and a sister who are twins; the heroine is a
girl who dresses up as a boy and, by the end of the play, many
of the characters have married someone they would not have
married at the beginning. The real comedy of the play, however,
does not lie in the main story, or **plot**, but in the **subplot**. The play
takes place mainly in the home of Olivia, a wealthy young
widow. Her steward, Malvolio, who is responsible for managing
her home, is a man with no sense of humour. He is so stern and
serious that he has offended many people, including Olivia's
servant Maria and her uncle, Sir Toby Belch, who is almost
always drunk. Sir Toby's friend, Sir Andrew Aguecheek, is
desperately in love with Olivia but he is a fool.

As always, Shakespeare shows us this early in the play. Sir Andrew first appears when Sir Toby and Maria are talking:

Sir Andrew:	*Sir Toby Belch! How now, Sir Toby Belch!*
Sir Toby:	*Sweet Sir Andrew!*
Sir Andrew:	*Bless you, fair shrew.*
	(He is speaking to Maria)
Maria:	*And you too, sir.*
Sir Toby:	*Accost, Sir Andrew, accost.*
	(He's telling Sir Andrew be brave and approach Olivia.)
Sir Andrew:	*What's that?*
	(Sir Andrew doesn't understand the word 'accost' so he asks what Sir Toby means.)
Sir Toby:	*My niece's chambermaid.*
	(Sir Toby doesn't understand Sir Andrew's question and thinks that he wants to know who Maria is.)
Sir Andrew:	*Good Mistress Accost, I desire better acquaintance.*
	(He is now totally confused and thinks that Maria's name is 'Accost'.)
Maria:	*My name is Mary, sir.*
Sir Andrew:	*Good Mistress Mary Accost...*

(Act I, Scene III)

ACTIVITY:

Read through this scene again and make sure that you understand all the words and can pronounce them correctly. Act out the scene in groups of three.

Because these characters don't like Malvolio, they decide to play a joke on him. They write a letter in Olivia's handwriting which seems to suggest that Olivia is deeply in love with him and that she would love him even more if he dressed and behaved in a certain way. Then they watch the poor man as he approaches Olivia.

Olivia:	*How now, Malvolio!*
Malvolio:	*Sweet lady, ho, ho!*
	(After asking him some questions and finding his replies very strange, Olivia thinks he may be ill.)
Olivia:	*Wilt thou go to bed, Malvolio?*
Malvolio:	*To bed? Ay, sweet heart, and I'll come to thee.*
	(Malvolio suggests going to bed with Olivia. She is very surprised!)
Olivia:	*God comfort thee. Why dost thou smile so, and kiss thy hand so oft?*
Maria:	*How do you, Malvolio?*
Malvolio:	*At your request!*
	(Here he answers Olivia's last question.)

(Act III Scene IV)

*'Some are born great,
some achieve greatness
And some have greatness
thrust upon 'em'*
Twelfth Night (Act II, Sc V)

DISCUSSION:
What do you think of Sir Toby's trick? Is it right to play such tricks on people? Can you think of any tricks which you have played on people?

Olivia asks Malvolio why he is dressed so strangely but she cannot understand any of his answers and decides that the midsummer heat must have made him mad, so she leaves, telling Maria to arrange for a doctor to examine him. The play now gets a little more serious because Sir Toby and his friends treat Malvolio like a madman, and they lock him up in a dark room. Eventually, of course, everything is sorted out, with only Malvolio left still very angry at having been tricked:

I'll be reveng'd on the whole pack of you.

(Act V, Scene I)

We have already mentioned that Shakespeare's plays became more serious as time went on. With this seriousness came a change in the role of the clown. This is very clear in the tragedy *King Lear*, but we can also see it happening in *Twelfth Night* if we look at the role of Feste, the clown. By the time this play was written (1601), Shakespeare's company had lost their old clown, Will Kempe, and had taken on Robert Armin, a much more philosophical type of clown who also wrote a play of his own and a book about fools and mad people called *A Nest of Ninnies*.

Here is Feste proving to Olivia, whom he calls '*madonna*' (my lady), that she is a fool:

Feste: *Good madonna, why mournest thou?*
Olivia: *Good fool, for my brother's death.*
Feste: *I think his soul is in hell, madonna.*
Olivia: *I know his soul is in heaven, fool.*
Feste: *The more fool, madonna, to mourn for your brother's soul being in heaven.*

(Act I, Scene V)

'O mistress mine, where are you roaming?'
Twelfth Night (Act II, Sc III)

He asks Olivia why she is so sad and she replies that it's because her brother is dead. When he tells her that he thinks her brother's soul is in hell, she replies that she knows it is in heaven. Then you are a fool to be sad for him, says Feste.

In the course of the play, Feste sings several very beautiful songs including a love song which encourages young people not to waste any time over falling in love because no one knows what will happen in the future:

O mistress mine, where are you roaming?
O stay and hear, your true love's coming,
That can sing both high and low.
Trip no further, pretty sweeting;
Journeys end in lovers meeting,
Every wise man's son doth know.

What is love? 'Tis not hereafter;
Present mirth hath present laughter;
What's to come is still unsure.
In delay there lies no plenty,
Then come kiss me, sweet and twenty.
Youth's a stuff will not endure.

(Act II, Scene III)

5. A GUIDED TOUR OF HELL

Queen Elizabeth I died in 1603 and was succeeded by James VI of Scotland, son of Mary Queen of Scots, whom Elizabeth had had executed in 1587. James, who became James I of England and Scotland, was a lover of the theatre and Shakespeare seems to have written a tragedy for him – *Macbeth,* which is set in Scotland. Before he did so, however, he wrote another tragedy, *Othello.*

James I

In his first play, *Titus Andronicus,* Shakespeare had presented a character of pure evil, Aaron:

If one good deed in all my life I did,
I do repent it from my very soul.

(Act V Scene III)

But now it is 1604, fifteen years after Shakespeare wrote *Titus Andronicus,* and he is at the height of his powers. The end of the Elizabethan age was not a happy time and his plays reflect that fact. The plague had come once more to London and, in an effort to stop it from spreading, all the London brothels (i.e. the places where prostitutes did their business) were pulled down. Shakespeare had become concerned with the subject of morality and, in particular, sexual morality. With Hamlet, he had given us a character who acted as a kind of guide for the audience, exploring a world where outward appearance concealed internal corruption. In *Othello,* he decided to attempt something even more difficult: he would show how an evil character can make an innocent person appear guilty.

51

Desdemona is a beautiful young girl who has fallen in love with Othello, a Moorish (i.e. from Morocco) general working for the government of Venice. Iago works for Othello, but he becomes jealous when Othello promotes Cassio rather than him and so he decides to take revenge. In this play, it is the evil Iago who acts as our tour guide, but this time the audience are taken on a tour of hell. This is Iago telling the audience what he plans to do:

Cassio's a proper man. Let me see now,
(Cassio is a good man.)
To get his place, and to plume up my will
In double knavery – how, how? – Let's see.
(How can I get his position and get pleasure from being an evil person?)
After some time, to abuse Othello's ears
That he is too familiar with his wife;
(I will lie to Othello and say that Cassio and Desdemona are lovers.)
He hath a person and a smooth dispose
To be suspected, framed to make women false.
(Cassio is a handsome man and even married women find him attractive.)
The Moor is of a free and open nature,
That thinks men honest that but seem to be so,
And will as tenderly be led by th' nose
As asses are.
(Othello trusts everyone, even dishonest people, and he can be easily tricked.)
I hav't. It is engender'd. Hell and night
Must bring this monstrous birth to the world's light.
(I've got it! I've made my plan! . . .)

(Act I, Scene III)

DISCUSSION:
One theme of this play is racism. Othello is a Moor and black. Desdemona is Italian and white. Many people believe that mixed marriages don't work. What is your opinion? What is the opinion of most of the people in your country? Try to identify positive points and problems of mixed marriages and then have a discussion on the topic.

Iago's plan is very simple. He makes Othello jealous of Cassio by making sure that Cassio will find and display a handkerchief which was given to Desdemona by Othello. Slowly but surely Othello becomes more and more convinced that Desdemona is being unfaithful to him. In Act IV, Scene I, driven to desperation, Othello tells Iago to get him some poison so that he can kill her. He wants poison because he is afraid that if he looks at her beauty he will be unable to commit the deed. It is in Iago's reply that we see the full extent of his evil:

Do it not with poison. Strangle her in her bed, even
the bed she hath contaminated.

(Act IV, Scene I)

'From the possession of this heavenly sight,
Blow me about in winds, roast me in sulphur
Wash me in steep-down gulfs of liquid fire!'

Othello (Act V, Sc II)

TALKING POINT:
In certain countries, there is a category of crime called 'crime of passion'. If a woman comes home to find her husband with another woman and they have an argument and she kills him – that is a crime of passion. If she devises a plan to kill her husband because she wants to get all his money, that is murder. A person will not be punished as badly for a crime of passion as for a planned murder. Does this exist in your country's legal system? Do you agree with it? If yes – why? If not – why not?
Is it possible to say that Iago is more responsible for Desdemona's death than Othello, even though it is Othello who kills her?

DID YOU KNOW?
The name Desdemona is a Greek word – *dysdaimona* – which means...unfortunate!

The tragedy of *Othello* is that we, the audience, know what is going to happen because Iago explains it all to us, but we cannot do anything to spare Othello any of the torture that he suffers. Act V, Scene II is the most terrible scene of the play, where Othello asks Desdemona to confess all her sins before he kills her. Of course, she has no sins to confess:

I never did offend you in my life.

but Othello is now so mad with jealousy that he cannot believe her and so, as she is begging for the opportunity to say just one prayer, he kills her.

Othello is a heartbreaking play, because almost all adults know what it is like to experience sexual jealousy. What makes this play so tragic is the innocence of Desdemona destroyed by the pure evil of Iago. At the very end of the play, when he is asked why he did what he did, Iago says:

Demand me nothing. What you know, you know.
From this time forth I never will speak word.

So Othello, who kills himself with a sword, never even gets the satisfaction of knowing why Iago destroyed his life. We do not see the death of Iago. At the end of the play, we are told that he will be tortured. Iago will suffer physical torture as punishment for the mental torture which he made Othello suffer.

ACTIVITY:
Read the following text quickly and
a) identify the titles of the two books mentioned and the names of the authors,
b) give the reasons why James I hated Scotland,
c) show how we know that James I loved the theatre.

6. THE SCOTTISH PLAY

The second part of the 16th century in England was marked by a large number of trials involving witchcraft. In 1563, the English Parliament had passed a law against witchcraft and many women were found guilty and executed. Not everyone believed in witches, however. Reginald Scot, an English gentleman, published a book in 1584 called *The Discoverie of Witchcraft*, in which he argued that ignorant people always blamed witches when something bad happened when, instead, they should blame themselves. Scot's book was not read by many people but, in 1597, a much more important and influential book was published. This book was called *Daemonologie* and it tried to show exactly how witches gained their power and what should be done to them. The author of this book was the man who became James I of Scotland and England in 1603! James I had been King James VI of Scotland since 1567 but hated that cold, wet country in the north of Britain which was always on the brink of civil war. He was a highly-educated, intellectual man who loved the theatre and almost the first thing he did when he became king was to double the fee which actors received for a court performance. This was the man for whom Shakespeare wrote his most poetic tragedy, *Macbeth*.

Macbeth opens in a thunderstorm with three witches discussing when they will meet Macbeth. They all say a line which we can recognize by now as being very Shakespearian: *'Fair is foul, and foul is fair.'* As in *Hamlet* and *Othello*, the audience is told that there is a great difference between appearance and reality. The witches meet Macbeth and his friend Banquo as they come from winning a battle and Macbeth is told that he will achieve great rank and become king. Banquo is told that he will not be king but that his successors will be kings. The witches vanish and then two men appear who tell Macbeth that the king, Duncan, has decided to reward Macbeth's victory by giving him a title of great rank – Thane of Cawdor, just as the witches had said.

'...I have given suck, and know
How tender 'tis to love the
babe that milks me:
I would, while it was smiling in
my face
Have plucked my nipple from
his boneless gums
And dashed his brains out'
  Macbeth (Act I, Sc VII)

In Act 1, Scene V, we meet Lady Macbeth for the first time and very quickly realize that she will stop at nothing to make sure that her husband becomes king. When she hears that Duncan will stay the night in Macbeth's castle, she says:

Come, you spirits
That tend on mortal thoughts, unsex me here,
And fill me from the crown to the toe top-full
Of direst cruelty! Make thick my blood...

She wants to get rid of her gentle female nature and be filled up with cruelty.

When Duncan arrives at Macbeth's castle, he says:

This castle hath a pleasant seat; the air
Nimbly and sweetly recommends itself
Upon our gentle senses.

(Act I, Scene VI)

DISCUSSION:
The theme of an ambitious man being pushed higher by his evil, more ambitious wife is a common theme in literature around the world.

Do you know of any books, plays or films with this theme?

What happens in the end? How do you think the story of *Macbeth* will end?

He obviously likes the castle, but we, the audience, know who and what is waiting for him inside. We have been warned by the witches – '*Fair is foul*'. Macbeth and Lady Macbeth argue about whether to kill Duncan but eventually Lady Macbeth persuades her husband that he must do it, and he does. They arrange the killing so that the blame falls on the two men who are guarding the king and, when the murder is discovered, Macbeth kills them before they can answer any questions. Several people are suspicious of Macbeth and leave the castle immediately but Act II ends with Macbeth about to be made King of Scotland

In Acts III and IV, we see Macbeth now trying to consolidate his position by killing all the people who could possibly challenge him. He remembers what the witches said about Banquo's successors being kings, so he arranges for Banquo and his son Fleance to be murdered. Fleance manages to escape but Banquo is killed. At a banquet held in his honour, Macbeth sees the ghost of Banquo and is so disturbed that he decides to visit the witches. He is given three prophecies:

a) that he should beware of the nobleman Macduff

b) that he should fear no one who was born of woman

c) that he will never be defeated until:

> *Great Birnam wood to high Dunsinane Hill*
> *Shall come against him.*
>
> *(Act IV, Scene I)*

Macbeth is very happy because it seems impossible to him that anyone could be born who was not '*born of woman*' and even more impossible that a huge forest could move. But the audience remembers the witches' '*Fair is foul*' – what appears good news may be very bad news. . . Before he leaves the witches, Macbeth asks about whether Banquo's children will ever be kings of Scotland. The vision he sees is the ghost of Banquo pointing to a long line of kings, one of whom is obviously supposed to be James I himself, together with many of his successors. It is obvious that, here, Shakespeare is including something that will please King James, who was himself traditionally supposed to have been the descendant of Banquo. Macbeth is very unhappy but acts immediately by ordering the murder of Macduff's wife and children.

In Act V, we witness the tragic end of Macbeth. We learn that Lady Macbeth is mentally ill. When we meet her, we realize that her conscience has at last caught up with her and she is suffering for all the evil she has done:

Here's the smell of the blood still. All the
Perfumes of Arabia will not sweeten this little hand.
O, o, o!

(Act V, Scene 1)

It comes as no surprise when we hear, with Macbeth, that she is dead. It is on hearing this news that Macbeth makes an intensely powerful speech:

Seyton: *The Queen, my lord, is dead.*
Macbeth: *She should have died hereafter.*
           There would have been a time for such a word.
           Tomorrow, and tomorrow, and tomorrow,
           Creeps in this petty pace from day to day
           To the last syllable of recorded time,
           And all our yesterdays have lighted fools
           The way to dusty death. Out, out, brief candle.
           Life's but a walking shadow, a poor player
           That struts and frets his hour upon the stage,
           And then is heard no more. It is a tale
           Told by an idiot, full of sound and fury,
           Signifying nothing.

(Act V, Scene IV)

DID YOU KNOW?
Actors are very superstitious people and believe that *Macbeth* is a very unlucky play. When they are talking about it, they never call it by its name but instead call it either 'that play' or 'the Scottish play'.

ACTIVITY:
This is a difficult speech. Work in groups to understand as much of the meaning as you can. Notice how Shakespeare uses imagery, in particular metaphors, to describe first time, and then life.

The end comes quickly now. A messenger reports that Birnam wood has indeed begun to move towards Dunsinane. (Macduff's men have cut down branches and tied them on to their bodies so as to hide their movements!) In the middle of the battle, Macbeth meets Macduff and warns him that he cannot be killed by any man *'of woman born'*. Macduff replies that he was not born naturally but that he was a premature baby who was *'from his mother's womb Untimely ripp'd.'* Macbeth is killed and Macduff brings his head to the new king, Malcolm.

7. SHAKESPEARE'S DARKEST TRAGEDY

In 1606, Shakespeare was 42 years old and a very mature and successful dramatist. He had seen his fortunes rise with the increase in the popularity of theatrical drama until he had become a wealthy man and a servant of the king; he had been married for almost 25 years and knew the joy of having children and watching them grow up and he also knew the pain of losing a child – his son Hamnet, who had been born as one of a pair of twins in 1585, and had died in 1596 at the age of 11. He must have seen much more cruelty, suffering, disease and death than we do today. We know all of these things about the man called William Shakespeare but what we will never know is how he could have written what is perhaps the greatest play in the world – *King Lear*.

The story of an old king of England and his three daughters was not invented by Shakespeare. He hardly ever invented the plot of his plays. For his Roman history plays like *Julius Caesar* he borrowed the story line from the Roman writer, Plutarch, whose writings were translated into English in 1579. For his British plays, like *Henry IV, Henry V, Richard III,* etc., he used a book of history, published in 1577, called *The Chronicles of England, Scotland and Ireland*, part of which was written by a man called Holinshed. The story of old King Lear appears in Holinshed's *Chronicles* and there was also a play entitled *The True Chronicle History of King Leir* which was printed in 1605.

Although Shakespeare may have borrowed the plot for *King Lear,* he turned it into one of the darkest, most tragic plays ever written. Like all of his tragedies, the story is very simple. In fact, in the beginning, it is almost like a children's fairy tale. An old king plans to divide up his kingdom between his three daughters according to how much each of them says they love him. The older two, Goneril and Regan, flatter their father by saying things which are not true but which the old man wants to hear and so he gives each of them large parts of the kingdom. Then comes the turn of Lear's youngest daughter Cordelia, his favourite. She says that she cannot speak falsely as her sisters have done so she will say nothing. Lear becomes angry, so Cordelia explains that she loves her father as a daughter *should* love her father:

You have begot me, bred me, loved me.
I Return those duties back as are right fit –
Obey you, love you, and most honour you.

(Act I, Scene I)

TALKING POINT:
Different societies deal with old people in different ways. Do you think that old people are well-treated in your society? Are they treated in the same way today as they were in the past? What are the advantages and disadvantages of having an old person, a grandmother or grandfather, living in the same house as their children or grandchildren?

But Lear wants to hear more. Cordelia refuses, so Lear gives her nothing and divides her part of the kingdom between the other two sisters. The king's wise old counsellor, Kent, tells the king that he is mad to act in this way, so Lear angrily exiles him, saying that if he returns to Britain he will die immediately. This all happens in the first scene of the play and sets the stage immediately for the tragedy that is to come. By the end of Act I, Lear has already argued with Goneril and is going to stay at Regan's castle. It is very common for old people to behave in a strange way from time to time, sometimes becoming angry and acting like little children, and some critics have argued that Shakespeare is presenting in this play an exploration of a kind of madness linked to old age. Lear is a very old man who wants to know he is loved and respected. Gradually, this knowledge is denied him and he is left alone, an outcast. Kent calls him *'old man'* and *'mad'*, in his fickle behaviour, while Regan says that it must be *'the infirmity of his age'*. Lear himself at the end of Act I prays:

O, let me not be mad, not mad, sweet heaven!
Keep me in temper. I would not be mad.

'Poor fool and knave, I have one part in my heart That's sorry for thee yet'
  King Lear (Act III, Sc II)

59

By the end of Act II, Lear has also argued with Regan and leaves her castle to go out onto the heath just as a storm is coming. Again, the last words he says are:

I shall go mad!

The part played by the Fool in *King Lear* is very important. We have already seen how Shakespeare uses the clown/fool to show us an alternative view of the action of the play, but in *King Lear* the Fool has a leading role. Because he is called 'boy', we can assume that this role was not written for the older Robert Armin – a singing and dancing clown. The fool is there to provide a contrast – the King acts like a fool, the Fool acts like a sensible person. In Act I, Lear asks the Fool:

Lear: *Dost thou call me fool, boy?*
Fool: *All thy other titles thou hast given away;*
that thou wast born with.

(*Act I, Scene IV*)

You gave away all your other titles when you gave away your kingdom, says the Fool. The only title left is the one you were born with – you were born a fool. Again, this makes us think of an old person behaving like a foolish child.

King Lear leaves Regan's castle, rejected, and goes out into the storm with only his Fool and old Kent, who has returned in disguise to look after the King. Lear cannot take the strain of his daughters' rejection any longer and goes mad. Then they meet Edgar, the son of the Earl of Gloucester. Edgar's brother Edmund has tricked their father into exiling Edgar, who has disguised himself as a mad beggar. Shakespeare shows us a king who should have acted wisely but acted madly and has now become mad; a Fool who speaks like a wise man and a clever man who has disguised himself as a madman. Each of these characters is given their own type of language to speak which separates them from each other. Eventually, after Gloucester has been blinded by Cornwall, in one of the most terrible and cruel scenes in all of Shakespeare:

Go thrust him out at gates, and let him smell
His way to Dover

(*Act III, Scene VII*)

there is a reunion between Lear and Cordelia, and Gloucester and Edgar. It looks as though the evil of Goneril, Regan and

Edmund will be punished and that the play will end with the true, loving daughter, Cordelia crowned queen and Lear happy again.

That is, in fact, the way that the earlier play, *The True Chronicle History of King Leir,* ended. But Shakespeare had very different plans.

In Act V, the army of Goneril and Regan defeats Cordelia's French army and she and Lear are taken prisoner; Goneril poisons Regan in order to win Edmund; Edmund is killed by his brother Edgar and Goneril commits suicide. However, Edmund has already ordered the death of Cordelia and she has been hanged. Lear comes in carrying the dead body of his daughter in his arms and, before he dies of a broken heart, asks the eternal question that people feel when someone they love has died:

Why should a dog, a horse, a rat, have life,
And thou no breath at all?. Thou'lt come no more.
Never, never, never, never, never.

(Act V, Scene III)

DID YOU KNOW?
By the end of the 17th century, people refused to accept Shakespeare's ending for the play because it was too sad. A dramatist called Nahum Tate rewrote the ending so that Lear got his kingdom back and Cordelia married Edgar. It was not until 1838 that Shakespeare's play was performed as he had written it. That means that nobody in 18th-century Britain saw the real *King Lear* performed.

King Lear is not an easy play. It offers no comfort. Although we see evil defeated, we also see goodness being destroyed. The suffering of Lear himself is the centre of the whole play; through his madness he occasionally glimpses truths of human existence. This is what makes Lear such a great tragic hero and *King Lear* the greatest of all Shakespeare's tragedies.

ACTIVITY:
Complete the following sentences:

a) *The saddest colour is*
c) *The saddest words you can hear are*
d) *The saddest thing that can happen is*
e) *The saddest person in the world is the person who*
f) *The saddest thing I've ever seen was*

Now work with a partner. Read what your partner has written and discuss your responses.

8. SET ME FREE

ACTIVITY:

As you read the following passage, fill in each blank with one of the words from the list below:

moving	writer	there	wrote	that	all
	great	people	of	about	

Shakespeare _____ three more tragedies: *Anthony and Cleopatra* (1606/7), *Coriolanus* (1607/8) and *Timon of Athens* (1608), the strangest _____ the three and the most similar to *King Lear*. These are _____ great plays, just as we would expect from a _____ of Shakespeare's power, but we can see that he was _____ away from tragedy. *Timon of Athens* is a play _____ a man who realizes _____ there is no such thing as real friendship – he becomes a misanthrope, a person who hates other _____. There is no reconciliation in *Timon of Athens*, as _____ is in *King Lear*, between Lear and Cordelia, which means that the sense' of tragedy is not as _____.

Between 1608 and 1613, Shakespeare wrote five more plays: *Pericles, Cymbeline, The Winter's Tale, The Tempest* and *Henry VIII*. The first four of these together are called 'The Late Comedies' while the fifth was obviously specially commissioned by the court. By far the greatest of these plays is *The Tempest*. In terms of pure entertainment and beautiful poetry, it may be Shakespeare's best play. In *The Tempest,* Shakespeare says farewell to the theatre, to his friends and to the people who went to see his first play twenty-five years before and who had followed his career. In that sense it is a very sad play.

Prospero the magician and his daughter Miranda live on an island with a strange half-human creature called Caliban and a spirit called Ariel. We quickly learn that Prospero's brother, Antonio, took Prospero's position in Milan and sent him and the baby Miranda to sea in an old rotten ship. Miranda has grown up on this island and has never seen another human being apart from her father. Prospero arranges for Ariel to create a tempest or storm which drives the King of Naples' ship to their island. On the ship is Prospero's evil brother Antonio. Prospero first arranges for the king's nephew, Ferdinand, to meet and fall in love with Miranda, and then for the wicked characters to see the evil of their ways and suffer guilt.

'You taught me language, and my profit on't
Is I know how to curse. The red plague rids you
For learning me your language'

The Tempest (Act I, Sc II)

In Act IV, the magician Prospero speaks some of Shakespeare's most famous lines, lines which become even more meaningful when we consider that this is the master magician of the theatre, Shakespeare, saying farewell:

Our revels now are ended. These our actors,
As I foretold you, were all spirits, and
Are melted into air, into thin air;
And, like the baseless fabric of this vision,
The cloud-capp'd towers, the gorgeous palaces,
The solemn temples, the great globe itself,
Yea, all which it inherit, shall dissolve
And, like this insubstantial pageant faded,
Leave not a rack behind. We are such stuff
As dreams are made on, and our little life
Is rounded with a sleep.

(Act IV, Scene I)

Prospero has just arranged a dramatic entertainment (called a **masque**) for Ferdinand and Miranda by using his magic, but the words also apply to Shakespeare's theatre. Just as actors are like spirits who live only when they are acting other people, so all the scenery of the stage disappears when the play has ended. Prospero mentions *'the great globe'* meaning the earth but the 'Globe' was also the name of Shakespeare's theatre.

The play ends happily with Prospero giving up his magic, everyone leaving the island to return home, Ariel the spirit being released and Caliban left once more in charge of his island. The last words that Prospero says, this time addressing us, his audience, are:

Let your indulgence set me free.

Prospero - *'What is't thou can'st demand?'* Ariel - *'My liberty'*

The Tempest (Act I, Sc II)

9. THE END

On June 29th, 1613, the Globe theatre was destroyed in a fire. For Shakespeare and his colleagues it must have been a terrible time. They were shareholders who had invested both time and money into making the Globe the greatest theatre in England. He must have felt how ironic was the words he had given Prospero – *'leave not a rack behind'*. We must remember that none of Shakespeare's plays had been printed at this time. Many copies of the plays must have existed because the actors would have needed them, but some of these might easily have been kept in the Globe and destroyed in the fire. After half a lifetime spent in the theatre writing and acting, he may have felt the terrible sadness of knowing that there was nothing left – not even his beloved Globe theatre.

On April 23rd, 1616, Shakespeare died. The verse on his gravestone, possibly the last lines of poetry that he ever wrote, is very simple:

Good friend for Jesus sake forbear
To dig the dust enclosed here:
Blest be the man that spares these stones,
And curst be he that moves my bones.

COMPOSITION:
In this chapter you have read about many of Shakespeare's plays. From the descriptions, which play do you think you would most like to read and which play would you least like to read? Write a composition of approximately 300 words, giving reasons for your answer.

V
SHAKESPEARE THROUGH THE AGES

The Two Gentlemen of Verona as performed by the Chung Ying Theatre Company, Hong Kong, 1991

1. THE POEMS

Shakespeare first became famous not for his plays but for his poems. His first poems – *Venus and Adonis* (1594) and *The Rape of Lucrece* (1594) – were both dedicated to the Earl of South- ampton and were popular enough to be reprinted many times. However, it is his sequence of 154 **sonnets** which show his true poetic greatness.

ACTIVITY:

*Read the following sonnet and try to identify the **rhyme scheme** - i.e. if line 1 rhymes with line 2, write a, a; if line 1 doesn't rhyme with line 2 but rhymes with line 3, write a, b, a. Also, count the number of lines and the number of syllables in each line. Don't worry if you can't understand exactly what the sonnet is about!*

Sonnet CVI (106)	**Rhyme**
When in the chronicle of wasted time	_____
I see descriptions of the fairest wights,	_____
And beauty making beautiful old rhyme,	_____
In praise of ladies dead and lovely knights;	_____
Then in the blazon of sweet beauty's best,	_____
Of hand, of foot, of lip, of eye, of brow,	_____
I see their antique pen would have express'd	_____
Even such a beauty as you master now.	_____
So all their praises are but prophecies	_____
Of this our time, all you prefiguring;	_____
And for they look'd but with divining eyes,	_____
They had not skill enough your worth to sing;	_____
* For we, which now behold these present days*	_____
* Have eyes to wonder, but lack tongues to praise.*	_____

Now write a short description of the sonnet, using the information you have gained from the above activity.

The sonnet form became very popular in England in the last ten years of the 16th century, which is when Shakespeare seems to have written his sonnet sequence. He did not try to publish them; instead, he gave them to his friends to read. They were eventually printed in 1609. Many of the sonnets obviously refer to Southampton but some refer to a woman who is described as 'dark'. No one knows who she was and she is now known as 'the dark lady of the sonnets'. Most likely, she was Shakespeare's lover in London. (Remember that his wife and family lived in faraway Stratford!) Because the sonnets have a lot to say about sexual love and because Shakespeare wrote many of them for Southampton, some people have suggested that Shakespeare was homosexual. This is possible but it is also possible that he wasn't! We simply don't know. Shakespeare's sequence of sonnets is one of the greatest achievements in the whole of English poetry. They cover a wide range of topics and emotions, yet what makes them so wonderful is the poet's control over his passion. In that way, the formality of the sonnet form is rather like the Japanese **haiku**.

2. SHAKESPEARE CRITICISM

DID YOU KNOW?

Shakespeare's plays offer speaking parts for 1277 characters. The largest speaking part is Hamlet, who has to speak an incredible 11,610 words - almost 40 percent of the whole play! An English doctor called Thomas Bowdler (1754 - 1825) decided that Shakespeare's language was too rude for respectable people so, in 1818, he published his 10-volume edition of the *Family Shakespeare*, which contained nothing that was 'unfit to be read aloud by a gentleman to a company of ladies'. There is now a verb in English - 'to bowdlerise', which means to censor something so that it will not cause offence.

Shakespeare's friend and fellow dramatist, Ben Jonson (1572-1637), thought that Shakespeare was a great writer but that he was not disciplined enough. The first great Shakespeare critic was the poet John Dryden (1631-1700). For him, Shakespeare was *'the father of our dramatic poets. . .'*, and the writer who had *'the largest and most comprehensive soul'*. For Romantic poets of the 19th century like Coleridge (1772-1834) and Keats (1795-1821), Shakespeare was like a god. It was these poets who drew attention to the great quality of his poetry and, through them, Shakespeare began to be used as a model and inspiration for writers throughout Europe and Russia.

By the end of the 19th century, attention had moved to Shakespeare's ability to create realistic characters who were psychologically very interesting. A.C. Bradley's *Shakespearian Tragedy* (1904) treated characters like Hamlet and Othello *'as though they were real people'*. From 1912, when the first professor of English literature took up his position at Cambridge University, the 'Shakespeare industry' had begun!

Thousands and thousands of books and articles have been written about Shakespeare since then. His plays have been studied and written about by Marxists, Christians, atheists, Buddhists, Muslims, liberals, conservatives, feminists. . . His works are studied in schools and universities throughout the world. People have even counted the number of words in each of his plays – *Hamlet* is the longest play with 4042 lines and 29,551 words!

3. THE INFLUENCE OF SHAKESPEARE

When the Elizabethan theatres reopened after the plague in 1594, Shakespeare was the greatest dramatist alive in England. By the end of his life, his influence was already very strong on his fellow writers and has grown steadily since then. With the spread of English as an international language, Shakespeare's influence grew and grew. He remains very popular in countries like India and Pakistan. His plays have inspired operas like Verdi's *Otello;* ballets like *Romeo and Juliet;* classical music such as Beethoven's *Coriolan* overture and even a rock musical based on *Othello* called *Catch My Soul (1971).*

Romeo and Juliet as performed by the Royal Ballet

Many films have been made of his plays, both in Europe and throughout the world. The Japanese film director, Akira Kurosawa, used Macbeth as the basis for *Throne Of Blood* and *King Lear* formed the basis of his greatest film, *Ran.*

71

Akira Kurosawa's *Ran*

Japan, India, Russia, Africa, Europe, China, South America . . . wherever there are people who love literature, you will find a copy of Shakespeare's works. When Shakespeare's plays were first printed in 1623, his friend Ben Jonson wrote a tribute which has only become more true as the centuries have passed:

He was not of an age, but for all time!

A SIMPLE CROSSWORD

DOWN
 1. This is the season for one of Shakespeare's last plays. (6)
 2. Metaphors and similes are examples of this. (7)
 3. Ophelia's brother. (7)
 4. The king who goes mad. (4)
 5. Perhaps the most evil of all Shakespeare's characters. (4)
 6. He fell in love with Cleopatra. (6)
 7. The Scottish play. (7)
 8. 10. & 16. A very foolish gentleman. (3, 6, 9)
 9. The longest of Shakespeare's plays. (6)
11. The author of *The Spanish Tragedy.* (3)
12. *The Comedy of_____ .* (6)
13. The Merchant of Venice. (7)
14. One of Shakespeare's last plays. (8)
15. She was Queen! (9)
17. One of Cordelia's sisters. (5)
18. He attempted to rebel against 15. (5)

ACROSS
 1. The greatest dramatist in the world. (7, 11)

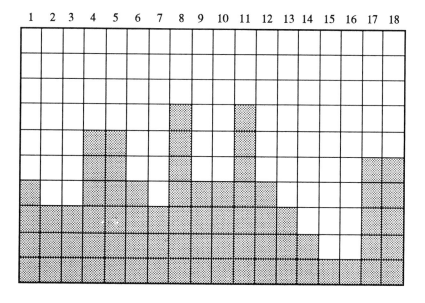

GLOSSARY OF LITERARY TERMS

blank verse
poetry which does not rhyme but which has a regular rhythm or pattern of stressed syllables

dialect
a variety of a language, spoken in one area of a country and likely to contain words not found in other areas

haiku
a very short Japanese poem of 3 lines and 17 syllables, arranged 5, 7, 5

iambic pentameter
the usual pattern of Shakesperean verse which has a weak syllable followed by a strong syllable, repeated five times, e.g. They 'had not 'skill 'enough your 'worth to 'sing

imagery
the use of images such as metaphors and similes to make a literary work more interesting

masque
a dramatic entertainment mainly involving dances and disguises (there is an important masque organized by Prospero in *The Tempest*)

metaphor
a type of image in which something/someone is described as being something/someone else, e.g. 'You are an angel'

plot
the story told by a work of literature

revenge tragedy
a very popular type of Elizabethan play in which a character is urged, often by a ghost, to seek revenge – Shakespeare's first play, *Titus Andronicus*, is a revenge tragedy, as is *Hamlet*

rhyme
a device used in poetry where two words which end in the same sound, e.g. day/say, are placed at the ends of successive lines

rhyme scheme
the pattern of rhymes throughout a poem

rhyming couplet
a pair of lines which rhyme – often used by Shakespeare to mark the end of a speech or scene

rhythm
the pattern of stressed syllables which occurs in poetry

simile
a type of image in which something/someone is described as being similar to something/someone else, e.g. 'You look like a dream'

soliloquy
a speech made by a character in a play but not addressed to any listener – it reveals what the character is thinking or planning to do

sonnet
a poem consisting of 14 lines with a fixed rhyme scheme. The Shakespearean sonnet had the following rhyme scheme: ababcdcde fefgg

stress
the pronunciation of a word or syllable with more emphasis than other words or syllables

subplot
the action of minor characters, usually in comedies, which is not directly related to the main plot of the play, e.g. In *Twelfth Night* the tricking of Malvolio is the subplot while the marriages of Olivia, Orsino and the other main character is the plot

syllable
a unit of speech, e.g. the word *syllable* contains three syllables: syll / a / ble

FURTHER READING

1. All quotations come from *William Shakespeare: The Complete Works,* edited by Stanley Wells and Gary Taylor and published by OUP (1988). The best introduction to Shakespeare is Shakespeare himself! Reading some of the plays discussed in this book is much better than reading about the plays.

2. The recent book by Peter Levi *–The Life & Times of William Shakespeare*, published by Macmillan (1988), is excellent and easy to read.

3. The recent book by Germaine Greer – *Shakespeare*, published by OUP (1986) in their 'Past Masters' series is very interesting as it discusses Shakespeare's thought and philosophy.

    There are thousands of books about Shakespeare's writing – too many to mention here.

ANSWER KEY

Many of the talking points and discussion topics are purely subjective and will depend on the individual's point of view. Where appropriate guidelines for discussions have been given but in general these discussions will reflect individual opinions. The aim is to promote and stimulate thought processes and there are no correct answers.

Some of the activities require essay-type assignments and answers are not appropriate.

Chapter I – The Elizabethan Age

Instructions page 3
1 Oxford
2 Birmingham
3

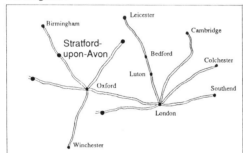

Activity page 4
The five mistakes in the picture are the:
. Coke sign
. bus stop
. TV aerials
. telephone box
. aeroplane

Activity page 7
The passage should be completed with the words in the following order:
came / born / became / was / developing / were / open / buy / sinking / begun / discovered / found / sent / conquer / destroyed / managed

Talking Point page 8
Possible reasons for performing *Titus Andronicus*:
. Historic – it is probably the first play that Shakespeare wrote.
. Social – it gives an insight into the lives of the people at that time. Violence and death was common.
. Artistic – although the play is violent, the language is beautifully written. Today we are frequently exposed to violent movies of very dubious artistic value as part of the 20th century media.
. Moral – even though evil seems to win over good - this is reality. Life is not always full of happy endings.

Activity page 11

b f a e d c

Activity page 12

1 C   2 D   3 A   4 F   5 E   6 B

Activity page 13

1 a In an attempt to cover up the terrible smell of death resulting from the plague.
   b Bubonic plague.
2 In order to prevent them spreading the disease to others.

Chapter II – The Elizabethan Theatre

Activity page 16

a True
b False
c False
d False   (men and boys performed in plays)
e False
f False
g False
h False

Activity page 18

Possible arguments to prevent James Burbage building a theatre near your home:
. noise created during the excavation and building period
. large crowds attracted to the area
. street hawkers selling food and drink to the audience
. drunk and rowdy crowds milling around after the performance
. thieves, prostitutes and beggars coming to the area to follow the crowds
. disturbances caused by fighting and quarelling inside and outside the theatre

Activity page 19

The passage should be completed with the words in the following order:
who / in / with / was / where / to / with / the / secretly / down / had / new /to / already / so

Talking Point page 21

It is possible that writers such as Marlowe and Jonson might have made good spies because they were well-connected in society and knew a lot of people. It would have been easy for them to infiltrate into many stratas of political, social and religious life without suspicion.

Good spies today need to be:
. ingenious
. clever
. discreet
. tactful
. cautious
. brave / courageous
. resourceful
. cunning

Chapter III – The Language of Shakespeare

Activity page 27

1
Positive	Negative
efficient	indolent
eager	lazy
thorough	complacent
industrious	lackadaisical
enthusiastic	unreceptive
dynamic	painstaking

2   The answers to this question are subjective and depend on the viewpoint and perspective of the student.

Activity page 28-29

a   the world is a stage / men and women are players = metaphor
b   quality of mercy drops as rain from heaven = simile
c   I'll be as patient as a stream = simile
d   soil has lips = metaphor
e   womb = kennel / child = hell-hound = metaphor
f   speak like thunder = simile

Activity page 29

1 c   2 g   3 b   4 i   5 h   6 a   7 f   8 j   9 e   10 d

Activity page 32

Summary of Mark Antony's prophesy:
. men's arms and legs (limbs) will be cursed (diseased)
. throughout Italy, families will quarrel and people will fight
. people will become so accustomed to seeing death and horror that mothers will only smile when they see their babies being killed, having no feelings of pity left
. Caesar's ghost will return, bringing war (Ate was a daughter of Zeus who incited men to do evil and to fight)
. all of this will be the result of the murder of Caesar

Activity page 36

There is no one correct answer to this, but note the following:
a   the main pattern in weak / strong / weak / strong, etc
b   however content words such as nouns, adjectives and verbs are more likely to be stressed than structure words such as auxilliary verbs, articles, prepositions, etc. and
c   words usually take a standard stress pattern in speech (i.e. the word `standard' has the stress on the first available, not the second).

So, for example,
    Over thy wounds now do I prophesy
would sound like this if the stress pattern were rigidly adhered to:
    O'ver thy 'wounds now 'do I 'prophe 'sy
but this would also distort normal English pronunciation - `Over - and also would stress the auxilliary `do rather than the adverb now. The line would sound better like this -
    'Over thy ' wounds 'now do I ' prophe ' sy

Comprehension page 38

1 a) iv
    b) iii
    c) iii
2 They all come from other languages.

Chapter IV – Shakespeare's Dramatic Achievement

Activity page 40

a) *Merchant of Venice* is difficult to classify.
b) *Richard III* was defeated by Henry Tudor.
c) No
d) 1603

Activity page 46

The passage should be completed with the words in the following order:
which / other / whether / be / could / that / by / never / watching / so / first / point / rather / price / didn't

Activity page 47

b) 1600 - 1608
c) *Troilus and Cressida* and *Measure For Measure*
d) moral behaviour / sexual behaviour
e) *Troilus and Cressida* and *Measure For Measure*
f) *All's Well That Ends Well*

Activity page 53

a) *The Discoverie of Witcheraft* – Reginald Scot
  Daemonologie – King James VI of Scotland (before he became James I, so James I would be wrong)
b) It was cold, wet and on the brink of civil war.
c) He doubled the fees for the actors performing at the royal court.

Activity page 62

The passage should be completed with the words in the following order:
wrote / of / all / writer / moving / about / that / people / there / great

Chapter V – Shakespeare Through the Ages

Activity page 68

line 1	a		line 8	d
line 2	b		line 9	e
line 3	a		line 10	f
line 4	b		line 11	e
line 5	c		line 12	f
line 6	d		line 13	g
line 7	c		line 14	g

A sonnet is a poem with 14 lines and 10 syllables in each line. In each group of four lines, every second line rhymes and the last two lines rhyme with each other (rhyming couplet). The rhyming scheme is ababcdcdefefgg.

Crossword page 73

Down

1 Winter	10 Andrew
2 Imagery	11 Kyd
3 Laertes	12 Errors
4 Lear	13 Shylock
5 Iago	14 Pericles
6 Antony	15 Elizabeth
7 Macbeth	16 Aguecheek
8 Sir	17 Regan
9 Hamlet	18 Essex

Across

1 William Shakespeare